JDV Philosophy Series - 6

INDIAN THINKERS

Modern and Contemporary Period

John Peter Vallabadoss

Jnana-Deepa Vidyapeeth

&

Christian World Imprints

First Published in 2020 by

Jnana-Deepa Vidyapeeth
Ramwadi, Nagar Road, **Pune-411014**
jdvoffice@jdv.edu.in
www.jdv.edu.in
Phone: +91 20 41036111

&

Christian World Imprints
Christian Publishing & Books from India
C-3, Wazirpur Industrial Area
Delhi-110052
cwidelhi2017@gmail.com
www.ChristianWorldImprints.com
Phone: +91 11 41526079

ISBN: 978-93-5148-426-4 (HB)
ISBN: 978-93-5148-427-1 (PB)

"Published with the help of the Institute of Missiology – Germany"

Printed in India.

CONTENTS

JDV PHILOSOPHY SERIES - 6

Since 1893 Jnana-Deepa Vidyapeeth has been pioneering philosophy discussion and debate inspired by prominent personalities like Richard De Smet, Jean de Marneffe, Salvino Azzopardi, Cyril Desbruslais, Noel Sheth, John Vattanky, etc. It has been in the forefront of promoting Indian philosophy and making philosophical thinking relevant for contemporary times. In its effort to reach out to like-minded scholars, JDV Philosophy Series has been visualized as a catalyst for interdisciplinary thinking and contemporary exploration on social issues fostering holistic liberation, integral development and creative engagement.

JDV Philosophy Series (Books published so far)

1. Salvino Azzopardi: ***Epistemology and Phenomenology of Religions*** (2018)
2. Kuruvilla Pandikattu & Thomas Karimundackal (eds): ***Melodies from the Flute*** (2018)
3. Kurien Kunnumpuram: ***Freedom and Joy*** (2018)
4. Cyril Desbruslais SJ: ***Postmodernity: An Indian Christian Philosophical Appraisal*** (2019)
5. Cyril Desbruslais SJ: ***Metaphysics Philosophy of Be-ing for Today*** (2019)
6. John Peter Vallabadoss: ***Indian Thinkers: Modern and Contemporary Period*** (2019)
7. Thomas Karimundackal & Kuruvilla Pandikattu (eds): ***Logic and Love***: For Prof John Vattanky SJ (2019)
8. Fabian Jose UMI: ***Relevance of Thomas Merton's Spirituality for the Consecrated Life in India*** (2019)
9. Kuruvilla Pandikattu & PT Mathew (eds): ***Committed to the Church and the Country***: For Prof Kurien Kunnumpuam SJ (2019)
10. Cyril Desbruslais SJ: ***The Philosophy of God for Today*** (2019)

INTRODUCTION
INDIA IN THE MODERN PERIOD

The encounter with other cultures from the time of Persian, Mughal and British invasion and rule was very much influential in shaping Indian philosophical and cultural milieu. Indian cultures and religions were forced to rethink and to open up to other ways of thinking and living. Especially, the British rule from the 18th Century brought deep socio-cultural changes in India. The changes led to a deep transformation of the religious and philosophical traditions of India. This process of transformation is rightly called 'Indian renaissance,' when various forces of change obliged the medieval set up to break down and brought the beginning of a new age. The fine background for modern and contemporary Indian thinking lies in the Bhakti movements and the revivalism of traditional popular religious traditions in the medieval period, especially in the central India, Bengal and in Tamil region. Much could be said about the medieval bhakti movements and their influence on Indian thought pattern.

In this course on Indian thinkers in Modern and Contemporary period, we will study the process of transformation as it appears in the life, activities and writings of Indian thinkers of the 19th and 20th century. The list of thinkers treated here are not exhaustive as we have only selected few representatives of certain type of thinking in each section. The following pages have writings on various thinkers which are merely a complied work (even reproduced) from unpublished study materials and class notes provided in JDV by professors like Claude Grou, Subash Anand, James Ponnaiya who have taught this course before the present writer. The credit of this work actually goes to them. We have merely added few sections of notes collected from other sources. Therefore, attention could be paid so as to consider this work only as a guiding material to lead students to go to original sources of the thinkers and study them deeply.

1. Context and Thinking

A familiar quote often used is that every thinker is a product of his/her times. Context of the thinker serves as a background or a platform for a person's world view. Close relationship, interaction and reflection with one's context, be it political, social, religious, geographical and historical, provide a stage for a thinker to come up with his/her idea. For Indian thinkers in modern and contemporary India the prevailing socio, economic and political contexts function as the platform to stand for certain values or reinvent ideas and values to adapt to new situation or to consolidate one's own traditional position. Continuous foreign rules, especially colonialism left a lasting impact in the modern and contemporary thinkers. Both the colonial and postcolonial periods have served as a context for modern thinkers in India.

We shall dwell briefly on the socio-economic-political situations of India as it turned a new leaf in its history as a modern India. Politically Indian sub-continent had been ruled from thirteenth century by foreign powers like Mughals, Portuguese, French, British. Local kingdoms in most part of India lost their dynastic rule except for some who remained in power compromising with the colonial powers. Nonetheless, strong oppositions from locals like Maratha powerful king Shivaji restricted the free expansion of Mughal and colonial powers. Towards beginning of eighteenth century, we find British gaining access to most part of India, gradually turning their commercial presence to political. Through a series victory and diplomatic policy of annexation the British gained territories. In 1857, a revolt in the army led to a confrontation between Indian *sepoys* and the British army. Though the British succeeded to calm the revolt, the episode led to a transformation of the political situation. The British crown took over from the East India Company, the government of India, dropping the policy of annexation and established a kind of diplomatic relationship with various princes of surrounding territories. India became the part of English imperial territory as British India, with exceptions of areas of Portuguese Goa and French Pondicherry.

2. Awakening of Nationalism

For many educated people, British rule was an improvement over the previous rule of Mughals. In the first of part of nineteenth century, we find a number of revolts against the British power. The revolts could be characterized as a slow but steady process, from isolated local resistance to national wide freedom movement, gaining momentum and acceleration till ousting of colonial powers from India for ever. In the western India, as British had taken over directly from the Hindu Maratha power, the reaction was quiet different. We find a growth of nationalistic feelings. In Bengal, a process of education that would lead gradually towards a formation of a nationalistic ideology had started. Foundation of Hindu college in 1818 provided English education to young Indians and exposed them to western ideas. After the *sepoy* mutiny 1857, we see a gradual change in the attitude of Indians. Many factors like, racial arrogance of the British, their disrespect for the Indian people, contempt of Indian customs, humiliations of Indians, non-accessibility of Indian to keys posts in administration, poorer economy of the country, cruelties and injustices of British, made Indians realize the need to start a struggle for independence.

Two models of nationalism seem to arise in the second part of the 19th century: Communal and Secular nationalism. Communal nationalism had its goal of reestablishment of a 'Hindu' or 'Muslim' rule in India. Whahabi movement was one such form. The continuation of nationalistic struggle of Shivaji had an ideology with communal flavor. In Bengal, under the inspiration of Bankin Chandra Chatterji, the movement had similarly a strong communal flavor. The secular nationalism tried to give a sense of its identity independently of its sense of religious belonging. Such nationalism found in 19th century Europe was seen to be the possibility for a nationalistic struggle in India. Ferozsha Mehta, Gokhale and Surendranath Bannerjee saw the nationalistic struggle in these secular lines.

The formation of Bengal British Indian Association in 1843, became the first effort to represent the Indian opinion. Later on the British Indian Association (1851), Indian League (1875) and Indian Association (1876) and finally the formation of Indian National Congress (1885) saw their role in terms of constitutional representation of the Indian opinions. They were dominated by moderate political thinkers. Yet revolutionary approach gradually penetrated, with the violent approach of Lokmanya Tilak and Aurobindo. There was a clear tension between the two positions, which led to the split in the congress in the 1906. After 1915, under the leadership of Gandhi the two groups united once again for the nationalistic fight. Still in this process the more extreme revolutionaries and those who saw nationalism in a communal perspective were left out.

When independence was obtained huge task of building up the nation on indigenous models was laid on its leaders. Post-Independence period have witnessed both continuity and discontinuity of what colonial powers have left behind. Emerging as a developing country, India has grown to be a matured largest democratic country with certain difficulties in the process. Without isolating itself in the modern world, India safely paraded and gained a respectable space for itself among the nations of the world.

3. Economic Situation

Due to the political stability of Mughal empire, the economy of India had a certain stability in 17th Century, when foreign traders entered India. With the gradual decline of the Mughal empire, struggle between rival powers, led to poor economic situation. Poor peasants had to pay for extravagant life style of princes and to finance their military campaigns. The middle class, made of traders and of servants of foreign companies, became oppressors of agriculturists. Different trade policies of foreign companies, especially the East Indian Company led to a further deterioration of the economy of the country. An economy based on colonial principles would eventually be a form of economic exploitation. At the same time, there was building up of an increasing middle class made of civil servants and Indian administrators. There was also a process of industrialization with basic capitalist economy. Initially the British capitalists benefited from it, but gradually number of Indian entrepreneurs profited in the field of industrial production. Impact of socialist democratic approach adapted by leaders immediately after the Independence led contemporary India to march forward with its various revolutions like agrarian, industrial and infrastructural. The private-public partnership in major growth-oriented areas had been largely proved to be successful. The economic reforms with foreign investment, liberalization and globalization have made India to be mapped among fast growing economy in the world.

4. Socio-Religious Situation

Religious and social rules were deeply interlocked in India. Norms of conduct were given a religious sanction and society was to a large extent guided by these rules. A society, guided by traditional rules of orthodoxy, led to traditionalism and stagnation. Although, there was a reawakening of Hinduism after the Maratha power, generally one finds clear signs of decadence in Hinduism at the time. A system of polytheism and idolatry was permitted even by the higher ranks of the Hindus who had Vedanta philosophy at the back of their mind. This distinction between a religion of high mystic and philosophical principles and a form of popular religion could clearly be seen; Vedanta as religion of the elite, and polytheism and idol worship as degraded form of religion among people. Popular religion was ridden with all types of superstitious and even immoral practices. Bhakti movements have contributed considerably towards blinding reason in favor of devotion and emotionalism. Caste rigidity got strengthened by unquestionable and unconditional love and surrender to the master, the Lord God.

English education started to have its impact clearly on society. Liberalism, rationalism and utilitarianism from English education had a spirit that challenged the very presuppositions on which the orthodox Hindu system of conduct was based. The challenge was not only to social customs, but on the very basis on which the social and religious structure stood. In the mind of British there was often a sense of superiority and a feeling that a native culture of India has not much to offer. Later along with growth of English learning, the spread of western ideas was much broader because of western type of learning introduced in vernacular. The official governmental effort towards English education was also accompanied by a missionary effort.

The British rulers, influenced by secular ideology, found themselves in a difficult situation when they had to deal with social reforms. Faced with obvious abuses in the name of religion they could not remain silent, on the other hand to interfere would mean siding with the reformers and alienating the orthodox group. After the mutiny, the Queen made a pledge according to which she would not interfere with the religious affairs of her subjects in India. Though the British authority in India was very careful in dealing with social issues linked with religious beliefs, it made it necessary for social reformers to show that reforms they proposed was not against the religion of the Hindus.

The reforms had three main categories: reforms to abuses of religious practices, reforms to the welfare of women, reforms to equality and freedom of people. First was related to some practices like hook swinging, which easily lead to accidental death of people. Reforms dealing with '*sati*', re-marriage of widows, child marriage, were done with certain governmental Acts and women education. Thirdly, reforms related to social inequalities in name of caste, untouchability and practice of slavery were finally and vehemently opposed by orthodoxy. Thus, new attempt at religious and social reform was guided by the liberal principles found in the contact educated Indians had with western ideas. The earliest expression of this new mentality is found in the work and writings of Raja Ram Mohan Roy and others.

In countering the superiority of Western ideas, the neo-traditionalists tried to unearth ancient Indian heritage and interpreted for our times. Using modern values of fraternity, liberty and egalitarianism, socialists and subaltern thinkers, vowed to condemn social discriminations and caste hierarchy. The post-independence period witnessed spectrum of thinkers like academic thinkers and spiritual gurus. The former attempted to be apologetic and emphatic in asserting Indian way of thinking and argued for a space for Indian philosophy in the world of ideas. The spiritual gurus and their new age movement have been successful in projecting Indian spiritual values to the West as an alternative to materialistic and technocratic worldview. In short, the socio-economic-religious-political context of about three centuries in the modern and contemporary period, serve as a background of Indian thinkers to build up their ideological base and legacy. Anyone who understands the specific context in which a thinker has emerged would be able to read him/her holistically.

Chapter 1

RELIGIOUS AND SOCIAL REFORMISTS

Introduction

Several contemporary reform movements introduced regeneration and reform in Indian society. They differed in their specific philosophies and generally stressed egalitarianism that does not discriminate. They advocated a return to the ancient egalitarian forms of life, and view the aspects of modern society such as social discrimination and the caste system, as being corrupt. Modern reform movements emerged in the 19th century India with the impact of the West on the East and as a challenge and response to this impact and the inter-cultural encounter. The reformists viewed Indian religion, culture and society critically and scientifically. British commercial and political engagement with Indian society contributed directly and indirectly to exam and assess the moral and intellectual condition of Indians. Above all their system of education in India paved the way for an intensive encounter of India with the West.

The western model of education offered scope for the intellectual and social uplift of India. The Western system of education and the rationalistic thought of the 19th century Europe provoked Indian intellectuals to be critical of their beliefs, traditions and social situations. It promoted also the discovery of the indigenous treasure of wisdom and Indian spirituality that gave the Indians an impetus to make serious studies of their own scriptures. They studied Sanskrit literature and found out the great discrepancy between the spirit and practice of the time. These enabled them to assert themselves and to bring their religion and society back to their pristine purity. A 'western impact' and an 'Indian response' could be traced in the renascent India. Hindu religion and society introduced a number of reforms and adaptations. Brahma Samaj and Arya Samaj were the notable religious reform movements of the Modern India.

1.1. Raja Ram Mohan Roy (1774-1833)

Raja Ram Mohan Roy was born in an orthodox Brahmin family in Bengal. He married in his early childhood and that too thrice before he reached the age of nine. His polygamous life must have made him later a strong opponent of child marriage and polygamy. His studies in Patna, the then centre of Islamic scholarship led him to the democratic ideals of Islam and the logical element of Arabic thought especially the rationalistic schools of Mutasilas. His studies on Islam made him strongly denounce idolatry and superstitions. The Brahma Samaj (One-God society) founded by him in 1828. It was the first modern religious reform movement which interpreted the Hindu scriptures and traditions to establish the universality of Hinduism and Brahma Samaj as the convergence of religions. On 27th September, 1833 he breathed his last in England.

Interpretation of the Vedas

Life of Hindus was regulated by strict rules of orthodoxy, embodied in the *sāstras*. Roy based his reform on a reinterpretation of *sāstras*. His method of interpretation had three objectives: A) *Building up a hierarchy of texts:* i. *Śṛuti* has preference over *Smṛti*. ii. Among *smṛti*, *Manu smṛti* has more authority than any other texts. B) *The role of Reason: Sastras* cannot go against reason. "The writings supposed sacred are only when consistent with sound reasoning, considered as imperative." C) *Spirituality over Religious rituals:* Roy subordinates the level of ritual actions to the level of higher religion. Legal aspect of religion is to be subordinated to the spiritual. These three principles offer a powerful tool to challenge the authority of the pandits and provide a ground for social changes. It reduces the laws to a minimum but it relativizes the whole scheme of law by submitting it to reason and by showing its relative character.

Monotheism in Vedas

Ram Mohan Roy's method of interpretation presupposes his faith in monotheism. He was convinced that monotheism was the only acceptable doctrine about God. For him, Vedas teach monotheism. His arguments are: 1. We find in the Vedas clear texts teaching the unity of God. 2. If the Vedas teach at the same time monotheism and polytheism there is an inner inconsistency and we cannot rely on the Vedas as a sure way to truth. 3. Since the Vedas clearly teach the unity of God we must give an interpretation of the texts apparently teaching polytheism that would avoid this inconsistency. 4. This interpretation is found in seeing these texts as allegorical. According to Roy, Vedas teach only unity of the Supreme. Various allegories were used to speak of the attributes of God. Later they are given concrete and independent existence, giving rise to polytheism and idolatry. This type of religion may be tolerated for uneducated, but it is not to be identified with the ideal thought of the Vedas. Roy had a tendency towards pure rationalism in his early writings, but in later times he did not want to rely on reason alone. He was conscious that reason alone cannot give us a sound basis for answering all basic problems of life.

Metaphysical Teaching

Conviction on Monotheism, had been mostly influenced by Islam, later developed in his translations of the Vedāntic texts. He claimed to follow the commentary of Śankara in his translation and interpretation of the Upanishads. Yet he differed from Śankara. For Roy, the absolute is unknowable. Man can know that it exists by reasoning from effects to cause but he can never know its essence. Some texts say that He can be known, others that He cannot. How are we to reconcile these statements? While speaking of unknowability of God, two other points are put forward by Roy. 1. The fact that God is the cause or creator of the universe. 2. The fact that we can prove the existence of God. The proof used is a primitive form of the proof from causality and of the proof from design. If one cannot know the essence of God, it seems however possible to come to a certain description of God. This description contains negative notes, denying every form of imperfection from God. Thus God is eternal, unsearchable, immutable. We can also speak positively of God. He is Creator, the author and preserver.

His interpretation of the Vedanta, gives a new turn, taking Vedanta away from absolutism and tending towards realism. "Maya implies, primarily, the power of creation; secondarily, its effect the universe. The Vedanta, by comparing the world with the misconceived notion of a snake, when a rope really exists, means that the world, like the supposed snake, has no independent existence, that it receives its existence from the Supreme Being." (*Works* II, 146). The Supreme Being and the world of matter together are eternal and uncreated. All objects take their origin from the universal matter under the supervision of the Supreme Spirit. Souls appear as particular expressions of the universal Spirit. The individuation is due to the connection with matter and vanishes when this connection ceases. The world, as Vedanta says, is but matter, the effect of Maya, and God is Spirit.

Roy rejects the possibility of God as the material cause of the world. Eternal atomic particles of matter are the fundamental material cause of the world. God is the efficient cause in bringing these particles together to take definite forms. His teachings evolved in the context of controversies. When he was concerned to assert the unity of God against idolatry, he was influenced by Islamic monotheism, and used Vedas and Vedanta. There he reinterpreted Vedanta in terms of monotheism. Later when in conflict with Baptist Missionaries, he defended all the *darṣanās*, overlooking the essential differences. Thus Atoms of Vaiśeṣika system was used with theistic interpretation of Brahman. As consistent metaphysics Roy's teaching is weak. He was a layman in philosophy and much of his philosophy evolves in polemics.

Idea of Religion

His religion was a syncretism of Rationalistic Hinduism, Islamic monotheism and Christian Ethics. He held that the supreme was to be attained through *Samādhi*- ecstatic union with God. *Samādhi* was promoted by means of congregational worship and mediation. He laid considerable emphasis on worship. His religion was to be a universal theistic fraternity, irrespective of caste, creed, and nationality. But individual religions should not merge into one; they form the embodiments of the universal religion.

Brahmo Samaj

Regarding the aim of the Brahmo Samaj, Ram Mohan says, "for the worship and adoration of the eternal, universal immutable Being, the author and preserver of this universe but not under or by any other name,' 'no graven image statue or sculpture, carving, painting, portrait or likeness, of anything shall be admitted within the message building, land, tenements, and premises, and that no sacrifice, offering or oblation, of any kind of thing shall ever be permitted therein. Hymns and sermons preached or sung shall be solely for promoting the contemplation of the Author and Preserver of the Universe, to the promotion of charity, morality, piety, benevolence, virtue, and union between various religions."

Creed of Brahmo Samaj

God is personal with sublime moral attributes; has no incarnations, hears and answers prayers, is to be worshipped only in spiritual ways; men of all caste and races may worship God acceptably; Repentance and cessation from sin is the only way to forgiveness and salvation; nature and intuition are the sources of the knowledge of God; no book is authoritative. God is the father of all men; all men are brothers; the soul is immortal and its progress is eternal; God rewards virtue and punishes sin; His punishments are remedial and not eternal. God is a trinity in unity. Brahmoism is the universal religion, it is God's latest dispensation and the missionaries are his disciples. The kingdom of God comes through inspired men, through nature, and intuition; God reveals His will on occasions to his servants by commands.

Socio-Political Thoughts

Roy considered the arrival of the British a blessing for India, as they enjoyed and promoted civil and political liberty. It is not fear but faith that allows for a stable government. A government which works for the good of the people and provides them timely justice has the trust of the people. The working of the government is regulated both by the parliament and by the judiciary. Hence the public must be consulted before any law can be enacted. The judiciary must not make any distinctions of the basis of race, religion or caste, but all citizens must be treated equally. This attitude deepens the emotional unity of the nation. The people must have the freedom to express themselves about the functioning of the government. Roy was a great apostle of the freedom of the press. When a nation can freely ventilate its grievances, then justice is better ensured, and the people have faith in their government. Suppressing this freedom leads to suspicion. By presenting the pros and cons of a case the press makes the constitutional process easier. A good press also educates the people.

One of Roy's great contributions in the field of social reforms was towards abolition of *sati*-the custom of burning widows alive along with corpse of her husband. Ram Mohan Roy approached the question of *sati,* as an ardent social reformer. He undertook the great task of refuting orthodox *smārtas* and their method of interpretation on *smṛti* in perpetuating the practice of *sati*. Immolation of the widow represents a non-progressive primitive type of mentality. It was erroneously thought to be rewarding both the widow and her deceased husband, as it cleanses of the great sin (*mahāpātaka*). He argued that no *śāstra* has ever sanctioned *sati*. He criticized it as 'deliberate female murder' and a perversion of Hinduism. Consequently, he collected funds for a society for the relief of the destitute widows to liberate them.

Ram Mohan defended also the right of women and condemned the polygamy of the Brahmins. The practice was abolished by Government of Bengal on the 4th December, 1829. He knew that a proper education is essential to bring self-awareness in the people and restore justice and equality. He fostered English education as profitable for intellectual re-awakening of the people and stressed the importance of a more liberal and enlightened system of instruction embracing mathematics, natural philosophy, chemistry, anatomy with other useful sciences.

1.2. Dayananda Saraswati (1824-1883)

While Raja Ram Mohan Roy attempted to reform on Hindu idolatry and polytheism from the left (Rationalism) in Bengal in the 18th century, Dayananda Saraswati did it from the right (Vedism) in Gujarat. His was a Rightist reaction. Dayananda was a radical religious reformer with the slogan "Back to the Vedas". His original name was Moola Sankar Tiwari, born in

1824 in Gujarat. Born and brought up in an orthodox Brahmin family he was disgusted with the idolatry, caste and child marriage and abandoned his home in 1845. At the age of 18 when he was initiated into the mysteries of Siva by his pious father in a Saivite temple, he revolted against idolatry at the sight of a mouse which defiled the statue of Siva. He left his father's house and became a wandering ascetic. In 1860 he found a guru Swami Virjanand Saraswati who was very strict and well versed in the Vedas. Moola Sankar underwent rigorous training under him, who gave him the name Dayanand. At the end of the training as Dayananda wanted to give him the *gurudakṣina*, (tuition fee, a gift) Virajananda refused it and extracted a promise from him that he would devote his whole life for the revival of Vedic Hinduism.

Dayananda was a *sanyāsi* who believed in the infallibility of the Vedas and cherished a very peculiar interpretation of the Vedas. He not only upheld the absolutism of the Vedas but also propounded the philosophy of dynamic realism. The Vedas contain according to him the seeds of all sciences and knowledge. His book *Satyārtha Prakash* (Light of Truth) contains his major ideas, interpretation of the Vedas and other religions. Dayananda undertook a tour across the country, condemned the caste system, idolatry, and child marriage. His theology welcomed the advances of sciences and technology. To him, the Vedas as the source book contained the seeds of science and technology. He initiated a number of reform programmes starting with a Vedic school in contradistinction to other public schools at that time in order to propagate and impart the Vedic values and religion to youth. He emphasized the theory of *karma* and *samsāra* and extolled the ideals of *brahmachārya* and *sanyāsa.*

Norms of Reform

Under the inflow of Western ideologies, Brahma Samaj followed the suit, proposing socio-religious reforms. India was becoming more and more aware of the value of its own tradition. The real question was how to answer to the challenges of the West without giving up our faithfulness to our own tradition. The criticism made by westerners, Christian missionaries and Brahma Samaj could not be ignored. No one could try to defend the actual practices of Hinduism. The defense had to start from an effort to purify it. This purification had to be done in faithfulness to the past, distinguishing the essential religion of India from the actual practices of Hinduism. Thus, is a necessity of new approach in interpreting the real meaning of the texts. We see a reverse movement: from Puranism into Philosophy, and from Philosophy into Vedism. 'Back to the Vedas,' was the motto of Dayananda.

Vedism

Dayananda wanted to reform Hinduism by returning to the original Vedic religion. He distinguished sharply between Hinduism and the Vedic religion which is the only true foundation of religion. He distinguished between books that have authority of their own and those which depend on other for their authority. 'All this is in the Vedas is true, all that is true finds its source in the Vedas.' 'Vedas are self-evidenced truth (*Swayam Prakāsh).*' Vedas are the eternal word of God and are an infallible expression of truth. All other texts have to be measured according to their conformity and non-conformity with the Vedas. 'The *Mantras* and the *Saṁhita* portion alone of the four Vedas are self-authoritative.' Thus, Dayananda excludes the Upanishads from the canon of infallible Vedic texts. In Interpreting Vedic texts, he found fault with modern methods of Indian scholars and western scholars. He wanted to go to ancient method. Two basic presuppositions of his method were: 1. Vedas are the eternal truth of God. 2. They teach the unity of God. The Vedas alone is the source of all knowledge, not the *smṛti*. There is no intermediary – priesthood-between God and Humans. An independent interpretation of the Vedas is the supreme audacity of man, and the greatest sin. We need to interpret the Vedas according to the laws of etymology contained in the *vedāṅga* called '*niruktā.*' Just as the sun needs no other light so too, the Vedas need no other book for its proof. It throws light on all things, but itself does not need any light.

Arya Samaj

Arya Samaj founded by Dayananda was a revolutionary social movement showing the falsehood of other religions and the purity and scientific background of the Vedas. Arya Samaj condemned idol-worship, animal sacrifices, pilgrimages, caste system, child marriage etc., and claimed to be a universalistic church. Dayanand attacked image worship, idolatry with all vehemence. He appealed to scriptures against tradition and cried, 'back to the Vedas.' Arya samaj has a two-fold mission; 1) to recall India to Vedism, 2) to preach vedism to the whole world. Arya Samaj set up schools and missionary organizations, in and outside India. The Samaj began to spread fast, and has today branches all over the world.

Religious Reforms

Dayanada was more successful in his attack on *Smṛti* tradition. He attacked the very citadel of Hinduism, the authority of the Brahmins. Hindus believed that though the Brahmin may not be a God, he is at all events, god-like, a subject not only of veneration, but of actual worship. He says, 'brahmins are not born, but qualified as such by virtue and learning. Brahmin is not to be adored. Gods and goddesses are not to be worshipped; only the Supreme Being is to be worshipped. God and soul and the world are distinct entities. They are related as the pervader and the pervaded. It is like the father-son relation; one is worshipped and the other is the worshipper. Caste is determined by merit and sterling worth. Wise men are the devas of the Rg Veda and the fools are Asuras. Deva puja is nothing but the respect shown to the wise. No ceremony is to be performed for the dead. *Yajna* or Vedic sacrifice is nothing but respect shown to the wise, parents, etc. They are done to purify the room, for the growth of plants etc. Though Dayanand's Arya Samaj was successful among the Hindus, it lacked the tolerance towards other religions and cultures and a universal vision and is criticized as a militant movement.

Chapter 2

NEO-TRADITIONISTS

Reform movement like Brahma Samaj had leaned on Western ideologies. The revival movement like Arya Samaj defended Indian tradition almost only in terms of the ancient wisdom found in the Vedas. Vedas were an absolute norm, codified in definite forms. This leads to a glorification of the past and a dream to live today the values of yesterday. Ultimately the movement had little true intellectual dynamism. It would contribute nothing to a new synthesis except a possible new interpretation of the past tradition. It gives value to one religious tradition, having a closed approach to all traditions. It was however possible to defend the Indian tradition in another manner, showing its own value, looking at a dynamic spiritual message not transmitted in academic circles but expressed in the life of saints.

2.1. Ramakrishna (1836-1886)

Ramakrishna, whose real name was Gadadhar, was born in 1836, at Kamarpukar, a small village in the Hooghly district in Bengal. His father was a village priest. As a child, he was subject to mystical visions, the first of which occurred at the age of six. He had an aversion for formal learning and he used to read the Hindu epics with great zeal. At the age of seventeen he joined his brother at the Kali temple of Dakshinesvar on the bank of the Ganges, four miles north of Calcutta. He became a *pujāri* at Dakshinesvar.

At Dakshinesvar, he felt a terrible longing for a vision of the Mother goddess (*kāli*), and he used to spend sleepless nights in a near-by-forest meditating on Kāli. The next twelve years was a period of intense spiritual agony and excruciating pain for Ramakrishna. Then came the first flash of immense illumination. The traumatic spiritual experience had tremendous effect on his thought, and behavior. He behaved at times like a mad man. His wife, Sarada Devi was only 6 when Ramakrishna married her. Soon after marriage, they lived separately for 13 years. Ramakrishna considered her as his Mother. Ramakrishna never lived as a house-holder. Sri Sarada Devi was his first disciple. From 1879 onwards disciples began to flock to him. He and these men renounced the world and became monks. The religious title *Paramahaṁsa,* (Supreme Swan) one of the highest given to a monk, was conferred on him. Ramakrishna died on August 15, 1886.

Ramakrishna, with his spiritual experience, provides a starting point for this new line in the defense of Hinduism. He appears as a living witness of the vitality of the Hindu tradition. Ramakrishna subordinated religious texts to the spiritual experience of man. Ramakrishna possessed great wisdom and knowledge. The most important source about his life and teachings, the *Gospel of Sri Rāmakrishna,* is written by his disciples. His cardinal religious tenet was *anubhava* (experience) and not *anumāna* (speculation), the hallmark of any religious person. He used to spend hours and sometimes whole night in prayer and meditation. Crying for God-experience he used to spend hours and days in front of the statue of Kāli whom he called the divine mother; thus he highlighted the once ancient Indian credo of the feminine aspect of God.

On Scriptures

'All scriptures and holy books, may be said to have been defiled because their contents have been uttered by the tongue of men; but what Brahman is, no tongue has yet been able to describe. Brahman is still undefiled.' He shows the radical limitation of scriptures, its total incapacity to say everything about God. It remains at the level of notions and never reaches the level of 'experience'. What really matters, is the experience of God and this can never be found in scriptures. Relationship between scriptures and the experience of God is like rain forecasts in the almanac and the rain. 'The almanac forecasts the rainfall of the year. But not a drop of water will you get by squeezing the almanac.' Scriptures are good in as much as they point out the way to God-realization. But, once this goal is achieved they become completely useless. 'They point out the path to reach God, after finding the way, what more need is there of them. They appear as mere dirt and straw.' Scriptures contain both things that are good and not profitable. They contain a mixture of sand and sugar; so one cannot take them as it is but find its essence–pure sugar, from a *sādhu.* This approach to scriptures dictates a completely different approach to the continuity of Indian tradition.

Sādhanās for God-Realization

Tantric *Sādhana* is practical, not bookish knowledge of tantric philosophy and religion. He met a tantric and was guided by her. This spiritual approach left aside the deformations and aberrations of *tantra,* not in a theoretical attempt to redefine the tantric teaching but just because only the highest spiritual teaching could be integrated in his spiritual quest. He could never be attracted by the erotic elements of the cult because he always saw the divine mother present in the Bhairavi or in any other woman he encountered. The three main elements of Tantric spirituality of Ramakrisha are, worship of the mother, practice of Kundalini yoga and practice of 64 main *tantras*.

Advaitic *Sādhana*: under the guidance of Tota Puri, Advaitic monk, Ramakrishna was initiated into Advaita. This *sādhana* is the path of knowledge and not of devotion. It consists in realizing Brahman by denying all that is not Brahman. This path is a path of constant negation, '*nēti nēti*' that leads ultimately to deny even the personal aspect of God to reach this Brahman. Advaita is identified with *jñāna* yoga. This path of *advaita* led him to an ultimate struggle of giving up the idea of a personal God.

Bhakti Sādhana: it is the Vaishnava path to God, Bhakti or love of god. God appears as a person to which the devotees can have a person to personal relationship. This is expressed in different manners in the vaishnava tradition. We have the peaceful love of the devotee for the father and ruler of the universe-*shanti bhāva*. We have the tender mood of the mother child relationship–*vatsalya bhāva*, as expressed in the image on Yasoda's love for Gopala. We have also the master servant relationship-*dāsya bhāva*, as in Hanuman to Rama. We have the friendship relation–*sakhya bhāva*, as in Arjuna to Krishna, and finally the model of intense passionate love-*madhura bhāva*, as in Radha and Krishna.

Among the three *sādhanas*, Ramakrishna did not seem to give great importance to *jñāna* yoga. He preferred the Bhakti as found in tantric and vaishnava traditions. "I don't want to become sugar; I want to eat it. I never feel like saying, 'I am brahman' I say 'thou art my lord and I am thy servant.' Ramakrishna feels that in *Brahma jñāna*, the 'I' disappears completely while in Bhakti, the 'I' remains as servant of the Lord. He does not want this *brahma jñāna*, 'I pray to the Divine mother, o mother, do not give me *brahma jñāna*.'

Rāmakrishna considered God as personal and impersonal and sought to experience him existentially. He advocated the theory that the life of a householder doing good works and the life of a *sanyāsi* by renunciation are equally good. He taught the harmony of religions and considered the many religions as the branches of the same tree. He advocated that social activities have value only if they help to the spiritual awakening of the self. His experience of Kāli, Sita, and the variety of experience of God according to the Veda, Vēdānta, Purānas and Tantras and the world religions convinced him of the unity and harmony of religions. His teaching can be summarised as realization of God as the core of religion and the ultimate goal of human existence. People with religious experience live in harmony, the absence of which generates fight, tension and dissension. Ramakrishna synthesized the ways of *jñāna*, *bhakti* and *karma* as conducive to the same God-realization.

Regarding the *Sādhanas*, he does not see one as truer than other; all are valid paths leading to God. However, his tendency is to favor the '*bhakti'* forms of *sādhana* and to see it as a better method of leading to God in this *Kaliyuga*.

Against Social Reforms

Being primarily concerned about personal realization, Ramakrishna spoke very little about social ethics. True, he was deeply sensitive to social injustice, but he was against social reform and uplift of the poor. It was his successor Vivekananda who brought the social dimension into Ramakrishna order, in imitation of the Christian missionaries and European social reformers and Hindu social reformers like Raj Ram Mohan Roy. Ramakrishna thought that social work might remove the moral effort of the person. Besides, according to the orthodox Karma theory, each one must work out one's salvation, and to help another might prevent him from reaping the fruits of his previous life's actions. Ramakrishna once asked ironically: "O God, please grant that I may dig a canal, build a school, and found a hospital?" This is exactly what the Ramakrishna Mission is doing today all over India!

Equality of Religions

If truth is one and if it can be approached form different angles, then according to Ramakrishna, all religions are equal. This truth is elucidated by various analogies by Ramakrishna. Truth is a reservoir of water, which a Hindu calls *jala*, a Muslim *pāni* and a Saheb (Englishman) calls it water. For Ramakrishna the different systems of philosophy and the different religions and sects (of Hinduism) did not teach isolated truths, but they all formed one synthesis, and he was a great harmonizer. By means of various *sādhanas*, he claimed to have realized the truth underlying the various philosophical systems and opposing religious traditions. He saw unity in diversity. A Vedic sage had said: "*Ekam sat viprah bahudha vadanti"* (truth is one and towards whom all are traveling, only they are coming through diverse ways). Here in Ramakrishna we have the beginning of the modern Hindu syncretistic tendency. By which all religions are reduced to the same level of value, both natural religions and God-established religions.

2.2. Vivekananda (1863-1902)

Vivekananda was born in a well-to-do family of Calcutta. His early life was not very eventful. In 1881, he happened to meet Ramakrishna Paramahamsa whom he accepted as his guide. After the death of Ramakrishna in 1886, he undertook an extensive travel of almost the whole of India. In 1893 he addressed the World Parliament of Religions at Chicago. After his return, he founded the Ramakrishna Ashram at Belur, near Calcutta. He breathed his last on the 4th of July 1902.

Being proud of Hindu tradition, he defended its value against western criticism. Using the Universalist approach of Ramakrishna, without rejecting non Vedic tradition, Vivekananda used a different pattern of integrating them in a higher synthesis. He saw various religious traditions as expressions of different religious experiences. There are various stages of the evolution of religious consciousness, like dualism, qualified monism and pure monism. Dualism is the religion of the masses, considering the world of change as real. Similarly, the qualified monism tries to save both the individuality of man and the infinity of God. Advaitic position is the ultimate philosophical position. Vivekananda was known for his Practical Vedanta and he attempted to prove the great Vedanta ideal in practical life. He believed in the basic oneness of existence and advocated strongly the eternal sameness or homogeneity beyond all differentiation, the unity of all personalities.

Advaitic interpretation

Reality is one absolute *Brahman*. Real is a 'whole' implying that there must be parts. But absolute is perfect unity, and therefore the distinction between parts and whole completely vanishes. The absolute *Brahman* is also beyond space, time and causation, and thus changeless. The changeless absolute is indeterminate without any attribute. However, the absolute can be described as *sat-cit-ānanda*. Love is the essential core of *ānanda* (bliss). Metaphysically speaking, reality is absolute *Brahman*, and the same reality viewed from religious point of view is God who is all-pervasive, present everywhere and in everything.

The world is one but appears as multiple due to *avidya*. Freedom from ignorance is by reaching true *jñāna*. Cause of *avidya* is the feeling of individuality and separateness. Concept of *māya* explains the world in relation to the Absolute. When the world is seen through the three categories of space, time and causation, it appears as a world of names and forms. A wave in the ocean is not distinct from ocean only in its form and name. it has no separate existence from ocean. Similarly, the phenomenal world is not unreal, is not a world of illusion. However, we give to it independent and absolute reality we misinterpret it. The rise and fall of world is in the absolute. The one reality appears in its 'causal form' or in its 'effect form.' A process of involution and evolution takes place. We cannot speak of creation in the strict sense but rather of a manifestation. The absolute is the manifestor of the universe. Everything is a projection of infinite intelligence. Ultimately there is only one soul that is the universal soul or *atman*. 'Every human being has a perfect divinity within himself.'

The picture of human that emerges in the philosophy of Vivekananda is an organized unity of the physical and the spiritual. Human is physically superior to all other animals because human's physical nature is better organized and exhibits a greater unity. This uniqueness of human's physical nature is also due to the presence of spirituality in the person. The true nature of *ātman* is identical with *Brahman*. The two are basically identical and their difference is only apparent. Normally we do not have an awareness of this identity, but certain experiences and realizations can be taken as pointers towards this. The most usual example is the feeling that one is capable of such an identity.

Liberation and the Means

The liberation can be attained through the practice of *yoga: karma-yoga, bhakti-yoga, jñāna-yoga,* and *rāja-yoga*. (1) In *Karma-Yoga*, work is not done due to compulsion, but out of a sense of duty. *Karma Mārga* is a system of ethics and religion intended to attain freedom through unselfishness and by good works. Man\woman has to remain in the world and has to keep on working as well as he\she can. A continuous doing of selfless work enables a person to rise above his\herself, and to feel oneness with everything which is nothing but the realization of immortality, the realization of oneness of everything. The *karma-yogi* works as a free being, unattached to all self-interest. Such work leads to knowledge, which in turn brings liberation. (2) *Bhakti-yoga* is a genuine search for the Lord in love. Love of God grows and assumes *para-bhakti* or supreme devotion in which all forms and rituals vanish. This is the way of knowing God through intensity of feeling. In *bhakti-yoga*, one trains to control one's feelings and emotions and gives the soul higher and higher direction towards God. Ordinary emotions can be converted into powerful feelings; ordinary love can be converted into Divine Love or Supreme Devotion. (3) *Jñāna-Yoga* explains the meaning of 'Thou art that' and tells human that one is essentially divine. The realization that bondage is due to ignorance is the basis of the way of knowledge. In *jñāna-yoga* the entire energy of the body can be concentrated in the direction of knowledge. In course of time this concentration will become more intense, and the individual may attain the stage of complete concentration or *samādhi*. At this stage, even the distinction between the Self and Brahman will vanish. It is a stage of perfect unity. (4) *Rāja-yoga* is the method of realization through the mystic union of the lower Self with the higher Self. It restrains the activities of the mind, and with the cessation of the activities of the mind, attachment and bondage disappears. Here the mind and the body are controlled by way of subjecting them to certain physical and mental disciplines. It produces certain super-normal powers, which the aspirant should ignore so as to attain liberation. When a person goes into *samādhi* or superconscious stage, one comes out as a sage and attains metaphysical and transcendental knowledge. Although, Vivekananda speaks of these four ways differently, he says that they are different ways for the realization of the same goal.

Practical Vedānta

Vedanta should not remain in the field of abstract philosophy but become the basis for a concrete attitude of life. Advaitic ethics rejects individualism, utilitarianism and dogmatic ethics. Advaita teaches that ultimately the individual has no meaning in himself. There is a fundamental unity of all beings. One becomes aware of self not as individual but gives up all forms of attachment to this individual self. This universal spirit of individual annihilation gives us a spirit of total openness. Seeing the need of social reforms and painfully being aware of the inequalities and injustices, he is for a radical transformation. The reform program starts with education, not the traditional education but rather a process of conscientization. People have to be made aware of the injustice in society. 'If the poor cannot go to class, education has to reach them at the plough, in the factory, everywhere.' To achieve this goal, he formed a group of dedicated monks. Teaching of Advaita would lead one to be aware of his strength. Thus, for him, spiritual liberation cannot come unless man is liberated from the slavery of injustice and poverty.

Towards a Universal Religion

Man finds in himself a deep frustration. He discovers a desire for the infinite and at the same time he experiences his radical incapacity to reach the infinite. He is bound in a world of nature preventing him to reach the infinite. Religion is an attempt to realize this. Ultimately religion is the realization of spirit as spirit. Empirically it is a process of man's struggle to go beyond nature and to live in the freedom of the spirit. Basic elements of religions such as philosophy, mythology and rituals are found in almost all religions. All these are good ways of approaching the absolute. 'All religions are good since the essentials are the same.' Harmony is possible because religions are not contradictory but supplementary. Ideal of religion is 'assimilation and not destruction, harmony and not dissension.' 'if we want to reach a real harmony we cannot be satisfied with an attitude of tolerance which is a passive attitude; we tolerate error and sin but we do not have to tolerate religions. A universal religion has the following features: (1) It must open its door to every individual who is free to decide one's religion. (2) It must be inclusive of all sects superseding conflicts and tensions that often occur among the various sects. (3) The spirit of universal religion implies acceptance. Acceptance is not just tolerance, which is negative in its import, but positive acceptance in which respect is shown to everyone. God is the essence and ideal of universal religion. (4) Universal religion has to be acceptable to all minds satisfying the largest possible proportion of humankind. Universal religion must harmoniously balance all the aspects of religion namely, philosophy, emotion, work, and mysticism.

Swami Vivekananda has revitalized the Indian thought. He identifies his thought with the philosophy of *Advaita* and gives the latter a new form. Brahman alone is real and the world is unreal. The body, life, mind, ego and the world are illusions. The Brahman is indeterminate, nameless, formless, eternal, existence, truth-consciousness and bliss. Every religion worships the same Absolute in different ways. Humanism is the dominant aspect in Vivekananda's philosophy and religion. The religion is expressed in service to humanity, universal brotherhood and humanism.

2.3. Aurobindo (1872–1950)

Aurobindo Ghosh was born on the 15th of August 1872 at Konanagar, West Bengal. He had his early education in the Loretto Convent School of Darjeeling. In 1885 he was sent to St. Paul's school, London. In 1893 he came back to India and joined the Baroda State Service, where he found enough leisure to read ancient Indian Philosophy. He remained in Baroda for about ten years, after which he devoted himself to political work till he was arrested in 1908. During his imprisonment he underwent a spiritual transformation, which took him to the ways of a Yogi. In April 1910, he shifted to Pondicherry, where he stayed till he breathed his last in 1950.

Integral Metaphysics

The real is non-dual and that this non duality should not be reached by chopping off elements of our integral experience but rather by trying to integrate them in a global vision of reality. Aurobindo is a non-dualist (advaitic), but different from that of Śankara. Maya is the real power of *Brahman*, part and parcel of consciousness. It is the creative power of *Brahman* who descends through it to the world of matter. There is nothing that is not permeated by *Brahman* and thus everything is real. The conscious is permeated by the unconscious and vice versa. Both the conscious and the unconscious are powers of *Brahman*. *Brahman* is pure existence and it is the very nature of the power of *Brahman* to manifest itself as the world of finite objects and selves. Universe is the power of *Brahman* manifesting itself. In the process of evolution, all beings constantly return to *Brahman*. This return to the primordial power of Being results in the evolution of the spirit into higher forms of consciousness.

Śankara's advaita reduces one basic dimension of our experience of reality to illusion. The absolute is *satcidānanda*, pure existence, consciousness and bliss. As pure consciousness the absolute is the supermind which is the alpha and omega of the process of creation and evolution. We have a downward process of involution and an upward process of evolution. This double process starts from and comes back to the supermind. Accepting the supermind as a creating power, Aurobindo can see the world as a real creation. Trying to explain creation he compares it to the process of ideation in the mind. The world appears as 'idea' in the supermind. This world appears as an expression of the cosmic play of infinite consciousness. It can never be reduced to a mere illusion.

For Aurobindo, all beings are the evolutes of the spirit. Every being has something in common with every other being. The ordinary distinction between the lower (plant) and the higher (animal) is not an essential distinction but only one of degree. The lower is constantly struggling to evolve into the higher, and the higher is always reflected in the lower. The universe is a constant evolutionary play between the lower and the higher, and the summit of evolution is the attainment of *satcitānanda*.

Evolution and Involution

He explains the decent of the absolute consciousness into ignorance. The origin of ignorance is in self-absorbed concentration of conscious force. Ignorance is seen first in the mind which is precisely the first expression of this concentration. Mind becomes the first stage in the process of descent. This first stage is the overmind. Here the supramental truth is veiled but its image is clearly reflected. From the overmind we pass to the stage of intuition, form intuition to the illumined mind, from illumined mind to higher mind and finally to the ordinary mind. The descent of consciousness does not stop at this level; we see a further descent of it in life and finally in matter. Reaching the level of matter, it has reached the last stage of descent, material nature, abyssal sleep, a fathomless trance of consciousness.

The movement of ascent: the process of evolution follows the same pattern as the process of descent but in reversed order, starting from matter and reaching to supermind and thereby sharing in the life of the absolute. The process has a triple character; Widening: simple forms of matter take an increasingly complex character so as to admit the concentration of a complex and subtle form of consciousness. Ascent: from lower to higher grade of being. Integration: as soon as the evolution reaches a higher grade, it takes up all the lower grades and transforms them according to its own principles and laws.

Integral Vedānta

In the prison cell he had a vision of the Absolute in all its cosmic dimensions. It was an integral vision of the Absolute or the ultimate reality. He experienced the one-ness of the prison cell, of the judge, the prisoners, and everything around him dissolved into an undifferentiated unity. This cosmic vision was the basis of the system of Vedanta, Integral Yoga, or the integral Vedanta. Aurobindo's vision was so vast and synthetic that it embraced the entire range of thought and reality; logic, epistemology, metaphysics, psychology, cosmology and theology, six classical Hindu systems Aurobindo's system is evolutionary in nature. For him, motion, development and progress are of the very nature of the Absolute.

His theory of Divine Dynamics reconciles dichotomy between matter and spirit, being and becoming. For Samkhya, Matter is dynamic while Spirit is static. Vedanta also taught the same doctrine. For the Buddha and Heraclitus, there is only becoming while for Aurobindo, Being is becoming. Yet, for Aurobindo, the motion of the Spirit and Matter is not mechanistic as in Darwin. It is an out and out Spiritual evolution. Aurobindo says that the Spirit is at work at every step in the evolutionary process. It is also a free movement of the Spirit. It is the play of the spirit (*līla*) for his self-manifestation. It is a Divine game (*līla*).

Aurobindo's system of spirituality of philosophy is an ascending order of development and a descending order of self-manifestation. There are seven spheres in all: three of the Spirit and three of Matter, with the Supermind in between them. Aurobindo divides these spheres into the Higher Hemisphere and the Lower Hemisphere. The Higher Hemisphere comprises the three aspects of the Spirit; Existence, Consciousness Force and Bliss: *Sat*, *Cit* and *Ānanda*. *Cit* is not a static intelligence as in the Upanishads or Śankara, but a most dynamic, force, called Consciousness Force. The Divine descends into matter under the pressure of Consciousness Force.

The Lower Hemisphere is made up of matter, life and mind in an ascending order of consciousness. Matter for Aurobindo, is never-pure dead matter: it is nothing but the lowest manifestation of the Spirit, and hence, it is something divine. Aurobindo breaks the Samkhya, Platonic and Cartesian Dualism totally. The reason is that there is never a moment of time when the *Cit* is totally absent from it. The Chandogya Upanishad declares, "This whole universe is Divine" - *Īśavāsyam idam sarvam.* Aurobindo also rejects Sankara Vedanta, in which system the phenomenal world (*vyāvhārika satya)* is under-valued as illusory. Śankara's world is neither real nor unreal *anirvacanīyam* of ineffable. For Aurobindo, Matter is as real as the Spirit, since Matter is nothing but the lowest manifestation of the Spirit. There is real identity between the two for Aurobindo.

For Aurobindo, the homogeneous synthesis between Spirit and Matter is possible throughout the mediation of a hypothetical entity he calls Supermind. Śankara cannot explain the phenomenal world except through the hypothesis of Maya, and Christian philosophy explains the phenomenal world through God's creative act. For Aristotle, Nyaya and Samkhya, the world is eternal, i.e., the elements are eternal. For Aurobindo, the Supermind partakes of the natures of both Spirit and Matter. It is the intermediary between Spirit and matter. The Supermind brings about the descent of the Spirit into Matter and on the other hand, it raises Matter into the realm of the Spirit.

Integral Life

The purpose of human life is to evolve spiritually upward toward Supramental consciousness, and human beings have the capacity to help or to hinder this process for the rest of the human community. In essence, when an individual attains to Overmental consciousness, then Overmind itself descends to the level of human consciousness in a way that goes well beyond the spiritual accomplishment of the individual. The way in which a person participates in this process of Divine self-manifestation is through the practice of *Integral Yoga* which is the integration of spiritual practice with regular activity in the world. The aim of human life is to follow the path of the ascent to the levels of the supernaturals one after another, from Overmind to the Supermind and so on. At the higher levels there is no possibility of falsity at all as ignorance and consciousness are inseparable there. The overmind now and then passes onto mind some great truth which cannot be accounted for by mind. When human rises to the levels of the overmind and becomes one with it, one becomes a superman. The superman of Aurobindo is a yogi who has surrendered oneself to God becoming one with him. It has nothing in common with the Superman of Nietzsche. There is no conflict or strife for those who have risen to higher levels. There is complete unity without difference. Such an experience is integral knowledge.

The essential teaching of Sri Aurobindo is that humans are in a transition toward the final evolution. They would surpass their present conditions and rise to a newer life with abundant knowledge and consciousness. It would transform not only the personal self but also this cosmos. It would cause the dawn of a New Heaven and a New Earth, the Kingdom of Heaven upon the earth. *Sanātana Dharma* is the eternal and universal religion, which India possesses as a God-mission to be the guardian, exemplar and missionary of this religion. The symbolic way of basic spiritual experience is to be found in the Vedas. The surface level only speaks of myths and rituals. The experience of the fundamental unity of being is a basic spiritual experience. To reach this integral unity we have to go beyond the frame work of logical reason. We have to reach a new dimension of knowledge.

2.4. Tagore (1861-1942)

Tagore was born on 7th August 1861, in Kolkata, Bengal. He belonged to an eminent and influential Bengali Brahmin family. He was born and brought up as an aristocrat and a lover of beauty. He became conscious of his higher mission of bringing human beings close to each other and to God. Tagore ranks with the greatest seers, sages and the devotees of India, who valued human being above everything else. Under the influence of the liberal tradition of his family and the philosophy of the Upanishads, he developed a positive view of life and love of humanity. He died on 7th August 1942. Rabindranath Tagore is a religious poet. It is right to call him a seer, visionary or mystic. It is from his poetry that we know of his philosophy. He does not present his philosophy in an academic manner. His philosophical thoughts are scattered in his literature. The three great movements at his time, namely Brahmo samaj, reform by Bankim Chandra Chatterjee and the nationalistic movement had a deep influence on him. His poetry is deeply marked by the new spirit in religion. He had been influenced by Upanishadic speculations, Vaishnava devotionalism, western thinking and Christian teaching.

Search for the Absolute

His writings are marked by a quest for the absolute. From the beginning he feels that there is a basic current of unity, a basic force of life and harmony behind the world. The 'Thou' in *Gitānjali*, is presented as a Supreme person who stands beside me, whose strength can transform my weaknesses into strength. Although this 'other' is the companion of my life, he passes often unnoticed. Man fails to see him, yet man lives in a hope of a final encounter with this 'other'. This final encounter will be a moment of ultimate bliss. One might look into the temples of organized religion to find this 'god' for whom he longs, but the God is not there. It is why Tagore can say; 'whom does thou worship in this lonely dark corner of a temple with doors all shut? Open thine eyes and see, thy god is not before thee; he is there where the tiller is tilling the hard ground.' (*Gitānjali* XI). Lord is to be discovered in man rather than in the confines of organized religion. Tagore becomes more specific. The absolute which was first discovered as the force present in nature, then the force present in man himself is now defined as the 'supreme man'. Tagore will now speak of the 'humanity of our God or of the divinity of man the eternal. Before we try to conclude on the real meaning of these expressions we must study better Tagore's approach to man.

Man the Supreme

Tagore sees the universe as evolving from an initial light. Up till the coming of man, evolution followed the path of physical aggrandizement; man set the movement free to achieve greater perfection. What marks man as a man, is the gift of imagination. It is this that allows man to break the narrow barriers of his day to day life and to have a glance at the ideal that is, in a way, already present in him. Man can now see man the supreme, and see his life as a striving to achieve this ideal. First step is to assert his freedom from the world of matter; man must learn that he is no more a slave of his narrow individuality and of his biological needs. Going beyond this limitation man becomes sensitive to what is universal in him. Tagore feels that this is the intuition expressed in the teaching of the great sages of India; the presence of the universal spirit as immediately felt in one's own personality. When man goes down to the core of his own being he finds there a basic unity of being. This basic unity is not perceived as a unity of total uniformity, but as an ultimate harmony; this unity of harmony is experienced in joy and love.

So there is spiritual current underlying the whole universe and unifying everything in a unity of harmony. First it was seen as a force of life, later it is identified with the supreme man. This is neither as a theistic god nor abstract ideal. Man the supreme as a personification of the real force of life; this force of life is a conscious center of harmony, a center which expressed perfectly what every man expresses partially. Each man, in as much as he realizes himself, becomes more and more perfectly an expression of this conscious center of harmony. Ever personal center is called to a perfect communion with the center; in this communion there remains a distinction between each person yet a perfect unity of love.

Ethics: Realization of Man Supreme

Man should not bind himself with artificial forms of asceticism; what binds man is the duty to create both an inner harmony in himself and a harmony between himself and the world around. The first task is that of creating an inner harmony; Tagore compares this task to that of a music maker; he has all that he needs to create a musical harmony, yet it is his task and responsibility to create this harmony; 'it is for man to produce the music of the spirit with all the notes which he has in his psychology and which, through in at attention or perversity, can easily be translated into a frightful noise. In music man is revealed, and not in noise." The moral task of man is not complete by the creation of this inner harmony; man has also to relate to the world outside; he is called to create a harmony between his inner self and the outside world. Man is not only a music maker, he is also an artist, and his role as an artist is precisely to express this deeper harmony between the outside and the inside. Here ethics open on the field of aesthetic; when man tries to express the delight of this harmony between the inner and the outer world, he enters the field of artistic creation.

Nature of the World

Tagore is of the opinion that the reality of creation has given a definite view on the nature of creation. Though his account of creation has a humanistic significance, it is, more or less, theistic. God, being the supreme reality, is the basis of the universe. Here, the creation is said to be the manifestation or the expression of the Absolute. According to Tagore, God finds Himself by creating. The reason for creation is joy. Using the Indian concept of '*līla*' Tagore says that creation is the '*līla*' of the creator. He creates in the fullness of joy-just to find Himself in the place of joy. Creation is separate from the Creator, and is yet united with Him.

Harmony in Society and among Religions

The drive to create harmony leads man to live in harmony with other men too; this harmony will be based on the principle of love. In trying to see the conditions necessary to build a universe of love, we enter the field of social thought. When he became self-conscious, man became conscious of a mysterious spirit of unity which found its manifestation through him in society'. Man first discovers this unity at a more limited level, say the unity of the tribe; gradually his outlook is broadened and he thinks in terms of national unity; even this unity is not complete, if nationalism leads one to create walls between his nation and others; we have to break down all the walls so that all men may be able to see each other face to face.

Society's goal is not merely to provide men with the basic requirements for biological subsistence; it must guide man in the realization of his spiritual ideals and to live in a genuine spirit of love. Insisting on spiritual values, society should accept the positive value of modern inventions. Here Tagore is opposed to Gandhi's refusal of modern progress. According to Tagore, tools are like artificial limbs which permit man to continue to work and advance. With man the biological evolution is stopped; nature does not create new forms; it is now man's responsibility to create tools to go forward; in doing so he expresses the creative spirit present in him. But obviously, we have to keep these tools under our control, so that these tools are always a help in man's ultimate quest.

For Tagore, merely 'no-war' is not identical with peace, because according to him 'no-war' forms only negative aspect of peace. What matters to him is the positive aspect of peace, i.e. to realize spiritual harmony of human beings. Peace, according to him cannot be mere negative of war, but it should mean mutual understanding and sympathy among the people of the same nation, other nations and the universe at large. Therefore, real peace cannot be achieved by any instrument of policy but through the spirit of love. He has travelled all over the world preaching the ideal of universal peace. He believes that each race should be allowed to develop itself and at the same time a sense of unity should be developed in people, so that keeping their identities, the different races and nations can meet and unite with each other for the national and universal peace.

If the society is to break down the narrow barriers of nationalism to open the gates to a universal society built on harmony and love, in the same way the narrow walls of religion have to be broken down to give place to the universal religion of man. Just as the bound of social system is meant to help the individual to transcend society, the bound of religious systems is meant to help the soul to transcend all religious and reach the final freedom. Tagore's life is a good example of an effort to be free from all fetters of religions in a quest to reach the universal man. Thus, with Tagore's writings, we have a world-affirming idealism; a poetic vision rather than a philosophical system. Here is no effort to bring rational proofs of the validity of his vision; there is no systematic effort to show the coherence of this vision. There is a beautiful vision; a vision that accepts the world and leads man to commit himself positively and lovingly to this world.

Tagore has an anthropomorphic conception of God. The infinite has been conceived as the supreme human personality. God is the creator of finite selves and nature. Though theism has the dominant theme in Tagore's philosophy, the impersonal and indeterminate nature of the absolute also finds place. The creation is considered as the '*līla*' of the creator God. In other words, God finds himself in creation. While speaking about human person, he places more emphasis on the spiritual and moral aspect of human being. One of the notable factors of Tagore's philosophy is that he sometimes makes his position confusing. The inconsistency in his thinking is justified by the fact that he is, basically, a mystic and poet.

Chapter 3

NATIONALISTS

Modern Indian political thinkers gave a concrete context and direction to a nation's public activities and formulate its style and endow it with object. With a national aspiration to be freed from clutches of colonial powers, the political thinkers with their ideology and activism have spelt out their plan of action through their contextual thinking on nationalism.

3.1. Bal Gangadhar Tilak (1856-1920)

Tilak was born of a middle class family on 23rd July 1856, at Ratnagiri in Maharashtra. He got his Sanskrit learning from his father and higher education in Poona. His contact with many patriotic co-students instilled in him the ideals of self-sacrifice and dedication to social causes. In 1881, he started newspapers *Kesari* and *Mahratta.* He was actively involved in Congress and independence movement. He initiated celebrations of Shivaji and Ganapati festivals through which he consolidated Hindu Maratha consciousness. In 1908, Tilak wrote *Gita Rahasya,* a lengthy and detailed commentary on the *Gita.* In it he attempted to prove two contentions; first, that the *Gita* advocates primarily a philosophy of action rather than renunciation or devotion; secondly, that social or political action is the duty of all citizens when the nation is threatened by internal decay or external oppression. On 1 August 1920, he passed away.

Basic Tenets

Lokmanya Tilak sees his metaphysics as expressing the basic Vedantic teaching. Yet he understands Advaitic teaching as a world-denying philosophy. Its main message is not that the world is unreal or illusory. Its central teaching is that the Brahman is real and world is perishable. He showed that Indian approach to metaphysical questions is better than Christian metaphysics. Tilak was opposed to the approach of the social reformers to social problems. Reforms create frictions in the community and thus weaken the bond of unity. Unity is essential for political action. Reforms should be made not by laws of foreign rulers but by our people. He was meant for reform from within, by *dharma.*

Political Philosophy

Tilak represents the full tide of ideological activity in the Indian Nationalist movement. He tried to combat the hold of Western ideologies on Indian thinking and to find somewhere in widely accepted Hindu thought a philosophy of Activism which would bring Hinduism 'out of the books and the caves' and replace European ideas as the basis of social action in India. Sivaji remained a model of dynamism. Tilak envisioned an awakened Hindu crusade to break the power of Britain. He found *Gita* eminently suited to this role. He stirred Indian masses to resistive action against the Government. He recognized that the *Gita* actually advocates at least three paths of conduct, *karma, jñāna* and *bhakti yoga. Karma-yoga* is supreme and is enjoyed by the *Gita* for our times. He sought to be against contemporary 'escapist' Hinduism which offers the false ideal of renunciation of all worldly activity by the seeker after self-realization. So, his reinterpretation of *Gita* is towards demonstrating a philosophy of activism rather than quietism for modern India. Krishna's advice to Arjuna is that he must achieve justice by fighting in the interests of public welfare. The path of action must be followed by all patriots.

His famous political slogan is, '*swarāj* is my birth right and I will have it.' *Swarāj* – Indian independence is not achieved by prayers and petitions. It is identified with *dharmarāj* and Hindu dharma. Tilak rejects the activism of the West adopted by leaders like Gokhale, who believed in gradual social reform as a precedent to *swarāj.* Western-type activism is devoted merely to improving worldly existence, whereas *karma-yoga* is to self-realization through service to humankind. Politically *swarāja* meant home-rule. Morally, it meant the attainment of the perfection of self-control which is essential for performing one's duty, *swadharma.* It also had a spiritual significance as it meant the realization of spiritual inner freedom and contemplative delight.

Western democratic system is not what India needs. The government must be based on wisdom and not on money. He did not agree with Gandhian theory of absolute non-violence. Non-violence cannot be an absolute norm of behaviour. Violence cannot be used unless it has been shown that non-violent means are unable to achieve the goal. Although a defender of altruistic violence, Tilak never preached political murder nor did he ever incite anybody to commit murder as a political means. For Tilak three types of people are there in the world. Those who have the preponderance of *sattvika* elements in them prefer spiritual and moral contemplation and teach their fellow-men by their own example of virtuous living. Those who have *rajasika* element in them take to the work of political agitation and propaganda. Those who have *tāmasika* element take recourse to violent activities. He discouraged revolutionary and violent activities by the *Tāmasika* people. Only a man who has reached the moral level where he can act in a completely disinterested spirit can use violence. In this case it is not the one who uses violence who is stained by the result of the action but the one who, by his evil ways, obliges him to use violence. He said, "From begging to open rebellion, choose anything according to your ability and do it, but remember the supremacy of *swadharma.*" He accepted the legal methods of political organization and agitation.

Philosophy of Religion

Dharma is used in two different senses; first refers to religion as such; it is *mokṣa dharma* and second one refers to the path leading to other-worldly happiness. In other contexts, it refers to the limitation of worldly morality. Both have this in common that they create a bond; the first between man and God, the second between man and man. The moral level, *dharma* as morality, is purely relational while the second leads us beyond the realm of pure reason. We should not separate the two completely. If we see the link between the two we see that one's moral commitment to his fellow man is already a religious duty.

In his interpretation of *Gita,* we find that Tilak has not dealt with religion and ethics as separate issues. He holds ethics to be part and parcel of religion. Tilak demonstrates that overemphasizing *nivṛtti* and *sanyāsa,* blocks social progress. *Pravṛtti* and disinterested action are important. Tilak does not reject liberation but he would consider it without disregarding the claims of life here. In his opinion, to accept *jñāna* as a tool useful in attaining liberation and *bhakti* as a means to realization, but to discard action because, involving the fruit of action as it does, it impedes liberation, is to take a one-sided view of it. His treatment of religion and philosophy centers on action and relates to life here. The concept of a transitory, illusive world does not harmonize with Tilak's insistence on action even for the enlightened person.

Tilak was one of the greatest nationalist leaders. His life and work constitute a great heritage. He was a political realist, constructive revolutionary. Tilak was a political thinker and leader of his time, expounding the theory of nationalism which was a synthesis of the teachers of eastern and western thinkers. His nationalism had a revivalist orientation, to bring to the front the message of the Vedas and the Gita for providing spiritual energy and moral enthusiasm to the nation. His political theory and activity were meant to substantiate the nationalistic movement by a strong cultural and religious revival of Hinduism. By this he created vital foundations of an assertive nationalism.

3.2. V. D. Savarkar (1883-1966)

Vinayak Damodar Sarvakar was born in 1883 in great family of Chitpavans, as the second son to Damodarpant in Bhagur in Nashik district of Maharashtra. After his initial schooling at Bhagur, he went to Ferguson College in Poona. Vinayak from his childhood was given to lofty aspirations and was known to be an exceptionally gifted child. He owed his patriotic and poetical inclinations to his father. He began to compose Marathi verses when he was ten years old. Well-known papers in Poona began to accept his contributions. During the wave of fanaticism passing all over Indian in 1893 to 1895, the stirring descriptions of bloodshed and hatred fired the blood of young Vinayak. He could not rest without wreaking some vengeance or other on the Moslems for the outrages and racial insults they had inflicted on Hindus in Bombay and other places. His devotion to Durga from his boyhood inflamed in him prayers for her assistance for liberation of his land and his race.

When Poona began the hot bed of sedition and intense political agitation and awakenings, Vinayak was naturally inclined towards socio-political activities. His love for the motherland gradually increased in him. He dedicated his life to the mission of liberating India from the fetters that held Her in bondage. He carried forth the torch of his fiery resolves and set the youth of India aflame. He would organize a secret society, arm and equip his countrymen and fight out the grand struggle and if need be, to die, sword in hand in Her cause. The secret society of Abhinav Bharat was born with systematic propaganda and introduced Shivaji and Ganapati festivals in the village. Having a scholarship, he left for England for higher studies in 1906. Even in England he continued his revolutionary activities and set up a front organization named Free India Society. He was arrested in 1910 in connection with a conspiracy in India and sent to Bombay and after a long trial was sentenced to fifty years' imprisonment and sent to Andamans. Later, he was transferred to Ratnagiri Jail and in 1924 after completing 14 years in Jail in sub-human conditions with a shattered health he was released with conditions of not leaving Ratnagiri. He continued his efforts to bring unity in India, by his constant writings and speeches. All met with pain and frustrations.

He was not satisfied with the positive reform of Hinduism and his program of reform was more militant in nature. His spirit was aroused by the methods employed by Muslim Mullahs and Christian Missionaries to convert untouchables to their faith. He wished to prevent this and through his remedial '*śuddhi*' ceremony of reconversion he brought back the converted Hindus back to their religion. He later joined the Hindu Mahāsabha and became its president.

As a great linguist and writer, Savarkar wrote his famous book *Hindutva* in which he had given an interpretation of the term 'hindu.' "A Hindu means a person who regards this land of Bharat Varsha from the Indus to the Seas as his Fatherland as well as his Holyland." This conception of Hinduism revolutionized the Hindu thought world and aimed to bring all sections into Hindu fold. The Hindu Sanghathan movement gained strength through this definition. He wrote articles in *Kesari, Shradanand, Lokmanya* in support of the movement for Hindu consolidation. A lot of his literature reflects his aggressive personality with motherland, martyrdom, Hindu nationalism. He died in 1966.

Socio-Political Thought

Savarkar gave a nationalist revolution and anti-imperialism. He also launched a complementary and equally basic social revolution. The thought behind it was that the shackles of social customs were as fatal as political slavery. During Tilak's time there was a controversy over whether politics came first or social reform. Savarkar believed that social and political revolutions were two wheels of the same chariot. He turned Ratnagiri into an ideal experimental center of Hindu social reform with concrete program of Hindu consolidation. His writings were aimed at changing the Hindu ethos and on social symbols of Hindus like the cow, sacrifices, *Purānas*, *Manusṁṛti*. His philosophy of Hindutva was completely different from that of others. it was free of religion and nationalistic. He sought a transformation of Hindutva from spiritual to nationalist. His social objective was a Hindu mind freed from blind religiosity, spiritualism and unquestioning belief in the scriptures.

The premises upon which Savarkar's social thinking is based are social equality, a sense of justice and intellectualism. The very concept that a person born Hindu is by birth free of the bondage of inequality is a radical revolution. To create this fellow-feeling and to bring together and homogenize the Hindu society on its basis was his aim. The Patit Pavan Mandir he built in Ratnagiri was inspired by a feeling of social brotherhood and justice. He was unpopular in criticizing the excess of good qualities among the Hindus, such as tolerance and compassion. Speaking about religious tolerance he said it is good to respect the religion of those who respect your religion but this cannot apply to Muslims and Christians who keep saying that the eradication of Hinduism is itself their religion. He said only that compassion was worthy of respect and practice which was beneficial for human good on earth. Violence to the extent it was necessary for human good could not be avoided.

Hindutva

Savarkar was a commentator of Indian nationalism and the founder of Hindu nationalism. One of the dimensions of Savarkar's life mission is the politics of *Hindutva* and idea of Hindu India. His political thought was oriented towards two goals: Akhand Bharat and establishment of political *Hindutva*. He framed an ideological outline of Hindu nationalism and outlined the political history of modern India from the Hindu point of view. He spoke at Nagpur Hindu Sabha session that the Hindus were naturally not averse to the goal of organizing the whole country into a single political unity. For Hindus the already achieved political unity, Hindusthan was their home, motherland, fatherland, holy land and everything. His political *Hindutva* is an angry form of Hindu opposition to the Congress idea of new nation on a territorial basis including Muslims in the national mainstream. Savarkar's *Hindutva* and Hindu nationalism are ideological form of his nationalist philosophy based upon the ethos of a particular religion and its cultural moorings.

Savarkar had stated that *Hindutva* is the nationalism of this country. For him, the term Hindu contains the memory of the holy Sindhu upon whose banks the Hindu race was born and brought up, along with its sister rivers. The essential ingredients of *Hindutva* and of nationalism are one and the same. Hindus are a nation by themselves and it is not internal integrity but the distinction from other social groups that gives particular society recognition as a nation. For him, the future of the Hindus is far more emotionally integrated with that of this country than of any non-Hindu. It is the Hindus who can be the bedrock of Indian nationalism. The strengthening and freedom of Hindu nation would mean the strengthening and freedom of the Indian nation. Organizing the Hindus would be helpful for organizing the Indian nation. Clarifying that the concept of the Hindu nation is not antithetical to the concept of an Indian nation, he said in 1965, "My India would be a democratic state in which people belonging to different religions, sects or races would be treated with perfect equality. None would be allowed to dominate others. None would be deprived of his just and equal rights of free citizenship so long as everyone discharged the common obligation which he owed to the state as a whole."

Conversion and *Śuddhi*

During his propagation of Hindutva he emphatically stated that change of religion meant change of nationhood. For him numbers constitute strength and there is a certain balance in the population of this country and it needs to be preserved. He held that one who changes his religion also changed his culture. The proselytization carried on by Christians and Muslims weans the people away from the cultural mainstream of this nation, and ultimately they no longer remain a part of the nation. A sort of aloofness, separatism, is born in the minds of the converted.

In his state-craft Savarkar laid down his national policy with these following premises: Hinduization of politics with consolidating Hindu consciousness; Militarization of Hindudom with establishment of organizations like Abhinav Bharat; later after disbanding Abhinav Bharat in 1952 he stressed on democratic ballot; every Indian must be a practicing patriot; building a homogenous society to create the Great Kingdom of Bharat. Savarkarism is a cultural nationalism and resorted to polarization of Indian society. V.D. Savarkar introduced the element of armed revolution into the struggle of Indian Independence. He as a leader of the Hindu Mahasabha worked for the motherland and aimed to achieve for Hindu Nation its proper and rightful place, for a free Hindu India. He was a maker of history in India and a writer who used history as a means of national awakening. He was a manifestation of the effulgence of *Hindutva*.

3.3. Gandhi (1869-1948)

Gandhi was born at Porbandar on the 2nd of October 1869. His early education was at Porbandar itself. In 1888, he was sent to England for legal studies. He returned to India in 1891 after qualifying as a barrister-at-law. After staying in India for a very brief period he went to South Africa in April 1893 to instruct the counsel for Dada Abdulla & Co. With his unique experiences of South African social and political adventures, he came to India to make efforts for its Independence by applying the method of *Satyāgraha*. After a few limited attempts at utilizing the method of *Satyāgraha* to deal with various injustices, he launched a nationwide agitation in 1919. Then he saw that people were not ready for a non-violent fight and he decided to suspend that struggle. After spending a long time in educating the people, he launched a nationwide action in 1930 (Quit India movement). After his confrontation with Dr. Ambedkar, he turned his attention to social problems such as untouchability and social inequality. In 1934, he left congress and withdrew from active politics. Back to the political scene in 1939, he organized a movement of individual *Satyāgraha* as protest against the war politics of British government. After the war, when India's independence was drawing near, Gandhiji was deeply concerned with the Hindu-Muslim tensions. At the time of independence, he went to Calcutta to try to avoid bloodshed and violence. Back to Delhi, he was assassinated in 1948.

Gandhi is not a philosopher in a strict sense of the term. Gandhi never attempted to present his thought in any single treatise. A voluminous literature has gone into studying the man and his thoughts. Besides, his own writings have run into 100 large volumes of published materials. They were all written on various occasions, in different contexts with diverse aims. That makes it difficult for many people to know his philosophy clearly. However, he had such an integrated vision which, he used not mechanically but creatively. His philosophy is derived from his basic vision of life and his commitment. This synthesis is found in his various letters, speeches and articles. There is a consistency in his thought, having a focal point on the concept of truth. Truth is at the center of his basic quest for knowledge (epistemologically) of his religious and metaphysical quest (ontological truth) and of his quest for a good life (moral truth).

Knowledge and Truth

If truth in itself is an absolute, truth is always perceived by man in an imperfect way. 'Finite being cannot know the absolute truth' 'relative truth is all we know'. Therefore, we can only follow the truth as we see it. No one can reach absolute certainty in this life. The quest to know 'truth' is an ever unfinished quest and life is a continuous 'experiment with truth' this attempt is done with faith and reason. Gandhi rejects vehemently rationalism or the theory that reason is the only guide to truth. Use of reason is to avoid every form of obscurantism. Reason is supreme in its own domain. There are fields where reason is not sufficient. Appeal to faith is must. Faith is understood in two levels; firstly, as faith-intuition which is a living, wide awake consciousness of God within. The other sense is more a social phenomenon belonging to the field of religion; faith as 'appropriation of the reasoned experience of people whom we believe to have lived a life purified by prayer and penance.

Truth and God

Gandhi speaks of two models of God: a theistic God and *Advaitic* absolutism. A personal God is the creator of humans who are to love and serve God. God and man are ultimately distinct realities. He is omniscient and omnipotent, as a judge of our actions. He speaks also God in monistic terms. God appears as an impersonal force or power as a divine law and as truth; God as a force: God is a living force. Our life is of that force. I perceive that while everything around me is ever changing, ever-dying, there is underlying all that change is a Living power that is changeless.' This power is identified with the law of the universe; 'God can be called by any other name so long as it connotes the living law of life.' God as Truth: Gandhi agreed that God is love; but he felt that the word love is used in many ways and can be ambiguous so he prefers to say god is truth. 'God is truth', 'is' certainly does not mean 'equal to' nor does it merely mean 'is truthful' truth is not a mere attribute of God, but he is that. He is nothing if he is not that. Truth is *sat, sat* means 'is'. Therefore truth is implied in 'is'. Later Gandhi says he would go a step further and say not only that God is truth but also that Truth is God. If the statement God is truth is a statement of absolute identity as the previous explanation suggests, the second statement does not add anything new; it only emphasizes the absolute identity and puts the stress on the absolute character of Truth.

Man and the World

He accepts the main features of the Hindu tradition; man has an immortal soul which is nothing but a drop in the total current of life. This immortal soul is found in a body. This body must be strong to give strength to the soul, but it must also be subdued. The goal of the soul is to be freed from the body as long as one does not reach liberation they should come back in new bodies after the death of the body. Rationality differentiates humans from animals. He is able to worship God and to be human is to live according to the law of non-violence and to abandon the law of the brutes.

Philosophy of Religion

Gandhi as a Hindu, found it to be suited for him, with its open, tolerant and non-violent attitude. He was critical of untouchability in the system and the norm of infallibility of the scriptures. His religious experience is in an indefinable mysterious power which is felt by men, but escapes 'proof' and literal intellectual formulation. Truth is God and truth is the ultimate goal of religions. Religion is a quest for truth. This truth is revealed in all the great religions of humanity and therefore these religions are true although they all embody this truth in imperfect human moulds. One need not only tolerate these religions but must have an attitude of positive love and respect towards them. Since all religions are equally valid paths to truth, one should not try to convert people from one religion to another.

Satyāgraha

For Gandhi, *satyāgraha* includes three basic values: truth, non-violence, and self-suffering. The purpose of *satyāgraha* is to bring an end to injustice by changing the heart of the wrong-doer by awakening, through love and self-suffering, one's sense of justice. Traditionally, there were two ways to deal with injustice: one either continued being a victim or one fought back with violence. Gandhi's ethical pacifistic nature would not allow him to be passive, and he was convinced that injustice corrupts the soul, both of the victim and the perpetrator. Hence, it would be wrong not to do anything. Fighting back with violence is no solution either since violence begets violence. In mutual violence, the original perpetrator of injustice would now feel victimized and thus justified in responding with violence. *Satyāgraha* was his alternative to both. He experimented with *satyāgraha* both in South Africa and India.

Looking at his various *satyāgraha* movements, one can discern a specific pattern. It starts with a careful marshalling of all the facts, leading to negotiation and possibly arbitration. One remains open to communication since each side in a conflict has only a partial view. Each side needs the critical perspective of the other to sort out truth from untruth. In case, the arbitration fails, the *satyāgrahi* prepares the group for direct action without resorting to violence. One has to offer love in response to emotional and physical violence. Now the *satyāgrahi*, after announcing his direct planned action, persists in action, accepting all adversity, until the issue is resolved to mutual satisfaction. One can claim to have won only if one's opponent can also say the same thing. In this way, *satyāgraha* is a new form of conflict resolution which can be applied to conflict between nations, between oppressed minorities and their governments, between social groups, and even between individuals.

Social Economic Vision and Action

Gandhi's social action was aimed at the transformation of society based on two basic convictions: (1) All human beings are brothers because they possess the same *ātman*. Hence, to injure another is to do violence to oneself. (2) All human beings are fundamentally good. Given these convictions, one can understand why Gandhi was committed to justice and equality. He fought for equality of women and *harijans* within Hindu society. He aimed at *Sarvōdaya*: everyone's self-development. He founded several *ashrams* where he gathered men and women of different castes and religions and encouraged them to lead a life of simplicity.

Gandhi's economic views were unorthodox, but he was against unbridled economic liberalization and material prosperity at the cost of human values. Economic policy should ensure that no one in this world goes hungry or homeless. He worked to create cottage industries and cooperatives in villages. The spinning wheel was a symbol of simplicity and self-reliance. He was also against welfarism. No able-bodied person should live on charity. Everyone must work hard to earn one's own bread. But, he did not believe in expropriation of the wealth of the rich since that would result in violence. So, he evolved the theory of Trusteeship in which the rich should act as trustees of their wealth, which they should use for social uplift.

He believed in the decentralization of power in which the base of political power should be small community groups patterned after the village *panchayats*. The state must have minimum power consistent with the aim of *sarvōdaya*, universal self-realization. *Ahimsa* should be the guiding principle of all political relationships. The term *Sarvōdaya* literally means the rise of all, i.e., a society in which the good of all is achieved. Gandhi writes about India of his dream where the goal of *Sarvōdaya* is achieved: "An India in which there shall be no high class and low class people, an India in which all communities shall live in perfect harmony; there can be no room in such an India for the curse of untouchability or the use of intoxication, drinks and drugs. Women will enjoy the same rights as men." From the writings of Gandhi five important aspects of *Sarvōdaya* society can be identified. They are, *Rama Rājya* (Kingdom of God), *Sarva Dharma Samabava* (secularism), *Swarāj, Swedēshi* and *Panchayat raj*.

The philosophy of Gandhi is a comprehensive system. His philosophy is not an abstract system of thought. Credit goes to him for blending philosophy with life, abstract principle with concrete reality of facts, religion with politics, and ethics with a program for social evolution. His system is a synthetic unity of different sciences. Humanism is the dominant principle in Gandhian philosophy. Gandhi speaks of two models to speak of God, namely, a theistic model and an *Advaitic* type of absolutism. He beautifully couples God with truth; he identifies God as truth and truth as God. The universe is considered as the expression of the absolute. Gandhi also finds the spiritual elements in the human being which acts as the basis of his/her dignity. Non-violent state characterized by economic equality can be considered as the essence of his political philosophy. In summary, his system is an exalted one in so far as he gives to mankind a complete set of social, economic, political, ethical and religious principles to govern the individual and humanity.

3.4. Nehru (1889-1964)

Jawaharlal Nehru was born on November 14, 1889 at Allahabad and educated in England, at Harrow and Cambridge. In 1912, Nehru returned home to play a central role in India's struggle for freedom from British colonial rule, and then, as Prime Minister of independent India for seventeen years, went on to shape the nation's future as a modern, secular and democratic state. He died in office on May 27, 1964. Nehru was visionary and idealist, scholar and statesman of international stature, and also an outstanding writer. His three most renowned books were, *An Autobiography, Glimpses of World History* and *The Discovery of India.* For Nehru, philosophy avoided constraints of religions and traditions and encouraged critical thought and inquiry. Yet it lived in its ivory tower and failed to link itself with everyday life and practical issues of human beings.

Nehru as a Political Thinker

Nehru is a political thinker who spelt out his seminal thoughts for reordering of a developing democratic society. His various writings, speeches, statements in Parliament, public platforms, international gatherings and elsewhere, contained a specific thought pattern of a visionary. Independent India was fortunate to have him as a thinker and leader to shape her future and guide her destiny. Due to his visionary approach and dynamic leadership India achieved in her infancy as an independent nation, greater progress and respectable position in the international sphere. Significant contribution of Nehru was his determination to draft the constitution of India for as secular democratic republic amid communal frenzy after the partition. His concept of democratic socialism and vision of modernity with planned development in fields of agriculture, industry, science, technology and atomic energy, put the country firmly on the road to economic progress. The non-aligned movement in international affairs enabled India to have cordial international relations and to contribute much to world peace.

Nehru as a Secularist

Nehru was a strong critic of communal politics. For Nehru, communalism is the enemy of Indian unity and integrity as a nation. He viewed it as another type of groupism in name of religion dividing humanity on primitive notions and faiths. Communalism advocates unholy and dangerous alliance between religion and politics. Nehru had little patience with religion in its communal manifestations. Religious communalism with its uncritical and habitual loyalty to communalized forms of religion is undoubtedly the biggest obstacle in the path of secularism. The constitutional reality of secularism cannot become a social reality until communalism ceases to be that.

Secularism is the only answer to the communalized society. His secularism is not secularism in the western sense of complete separation between religious authority and the state. It is not also with a spirit of antagonism towards everything that is signified by religion. His secularism is not opposed to religion as to exclude religion from human life. Secularism has a capacity to save religion by preventing it getting mixed up with politics and everyday affairs of a state. Only tolerance and mutual respect for every religion ensures safe governance of a country and growth of its people. Progress is put on hold in an atmosphere of tension and conflict. Nehru attempted a definition of religion ignoring its communal forms and turned his attention to what is noble and personal in it. It consists of the inner development of the individual, the evolution of one's consciousness. Secularism guarantees fully religious liberty to all individuals and groups and forbids discrimination against any citizen on the ground only of religion, caste, etc.

Nehru as a Democratic Socialist

With a vision of Nehru and Ambedkar, Indian Constitutional Assembly opted for the secular state in order to strengthen the foundations of democracy. Nehru stood for creating a classless society with equal opportunities for all. As a socialist he adopted the principles of socialism in the West and applied critically those principles to suit our Indian conditions. He was not for a socialism that totalizes state's authority and regulated human lives without rightful autonomy and freedom. He aimed at adopting socialist principles to go along the lines of democratic principles.

For Nehru the barrier of group and class had no meaning. He was above all creeds and dogmas and he disliked all which was static and hence he disliked those ideas which ceased to grow with the changing times. In Indian context, recognition of individual dignity was a major step towards socialism. Nehru wanted socialism to be a living philosophy which must answer the problems of today. His socialism was not a dogmatic ideal, but an ever growing and changing philosophy which molds society and in turn molds itself as and when situations demand. Nehru's socialism also has a distinct impress of Indian thinking. He saw a way out in socialism to eradicate poverty and emancipate society from many social evils. His socialism's ultimate objective was to achieve individual liberty accompanied by equal opportunities and equality among people, through the scientific theory of Marxism applied with Gandhian techniques. His love for socialism was responsible for expansion of heavy industries in the public sector.

Democracy was the only method by which justice would be assured to the large majority of the population who had not immediately benefited by independence and who continued to remain in conditions of deprivation. A democratic constitution ensured adult franchise and periodic opportunity for the people to register their views. Nehru's socialistic democracy denoted democracy with social justice or socialist planning based on democratic premises. For him, democracy and socialism are means to an end, not the end itself. Democracy without socialism leads inevitably to intolerable deprivation and social injustice. It leads to political oppression, economic stagnation and nothing less than the alienation of the individual in conditions of anomy.

Nehru as a Humanist

Corliss Lamont defines humanism as 'a philosophy of joyous service for the greater good of all humanity in this natural world and advocating the methods of reason, science and democracy.' Of the two varieties of humanism, liberal and Marxist, Nehru was much closer to the liberal humanism. For despite being influenced by Marxian ideas, such as the polarity of opposing forces, the Gandhian influence was so deep and pervasive that Nehru could not subscribe to the violence implicit in the Marxist view of conflict resolution. Especially valuable for him was Gandhi's ethics of ends and means, with its emphasis on right means as the only way to secure right ends.

Nehru's Foreign Policy and International Relations

Nehru as the conceiver and founder of Non-alignment. He was an architect of India's foreign policy. He kept up India's insistence of not to be imprisoned in the available straitjackets of the Cold War for conducting its external relations. Nehru's foreign policy was based on the considerations of long-term interests of India. He was a crusader of peace and believed that the security of South-East Asia depended on a policy of non-alignment. The main objectives of the foreign policy of India are all contained in the speech of Nehru broadcast on September 7, 1946. Its salient objectives may be enumerated as follows: 1. To develop contact with other nations and co-operate with them in furtherance of world peace and freedom. 2. As far as possible to keep away from power politics of groups, aligned against one another, which led to two World Wars in the past and may again lead to a disaster on a vaster scale. 3. To work for the emancipation of the colonial people and the welfare and progress of dependent people towards self-government. 4. To utterly repudiate the Nazi doctrine of racialism. 5. To work for one world based on co-operation of free people in which various groups shall not exploit each other. 6. To have friendly and co-operative relations with England and other countries of the British Common Wealth.

As a statesman and political thinker Nehru emphasized secularism and democratic values. The essence of his contribution to nation-building has been secularism, democracy, planned development and non-alignment. He showed that planning in Indian conditions meant socialism and that the democratic process and the socialist process should and could go together.

Chapter 4

HUMANISTS AND SOCIALISTS

4.1. M. N. Roy (1887-1954)

Narendra Nath Bhattacharya was born in 24 Parganas District, Bengal on 21 March, 1887. His parents were Dinabandhu Bhattacharya and Basanti Kumari. He joined the revolutionary movement in Bengal led by Aurobindo and played a prominent role in it. During the First World War, he left the country and changed his name as Manabendra Nath Roy and became attracted towards radical views. He was arrested by British but managed to escape and fled to Mexico. Having involved in Mexican politics he became General Secretary of the Socialist Party. His activities drew the attention of Lenin who invited him to Russia in 1920 for World Congress. He differed with Lenin on the colonial question. He came back to India and suffered six years' rigorous imprisonment. In 1936, he joined the Indian National Congress and his famous slogan was 'power to the people.' In 1946, he came out with his philosophy of 'New Humanism.' He expired on 15th January, 1954.

Views on Marxism

Roy's ideology of revolutionary nationalism, shifted to Marxism. Though he remained close to orthodox Marxism, he always had the courage to disagree even with a man like Lenin. He sees two main characteristics of Marxism: materialistic and teleological. He accepts the first and rejects the second. We cannot make historical materialism as deterministic. He rejected the idea that all changes in history are caused by economic transformation. Economic determinism and divine providence of traditional religions, have made humans victim of outside forces which are completely out of his control. He rejects also the theory of surplus value and class struggles. He rejects Marxian political theory where an individual is subordinated to the society. 'We find society is the creation of individuals. The individual comes first; he is prior to society. Society is the means of attaining the end of freedom and progress of the individual.' Marxism is totalitarianism, and classless society is a utopia. Marxist materialism is too narrow, which denies the autonomy of the human mind.

Radical Humanism

Root of Roy's radical humanism is in the theory of monistic materialism. Materialism is the only rationally acceptable answer to the basic metaphysical quest. Philosophy fell in the error of dualism; modern science corrects this and enables materialism. Reality is a whole which can be called physical nature. Man finds his place in this whole and finds himself organically one with the whole of physical nature. Materialism means precisely that human evolution traces its origin to the background of the physical universe. Man is the last and the highest expression of this unified evolutionary process of the universe. He has evolved out of nature as the end product of a long process. Man finds his place and meaning in the material universe. He has a privileged role since man is the measure of all things. Man is not subordinated to any supra human power. This rejects the hypothesis of God and the idea that in man there is some mysterious spiritual power. Humanism starts from the way man emerges in nature and finds its central idea in this that man cannot be subordinated to any outside force or principle.

A basic dimension of Roy's humanism is his rationalism. He believes that the basic harmony of the universe finds its echo in man's rationality. Man must be guided by reason and set aside all forms of beliefs and superstitions. Man is basically free. The concept of human freedom is as central as that of rationality to humanism. The quest for freedom is basic to man and is part of man's struggle to exist as a man. It is as basic to man as the instinct of survival in animals. The third dimension of humanism is morality. Morality is closely linked with the principle of rationality and freedom but it has to be developed as the basis of a system of ethics.

M.N. Roy was the embodiment of the vital force in pinning his undying faith on man – not in the abstract but as the individual measure of all things. He hated injustice and inhumanity although he recognized development and decay as inseparable from the process of life. His humanism is in his ideal of establishing life on earth as full and integrated in which both mind and body receive their just dues.

4.2. Amartya Sen (1933 -)

Amartya Kumar Sen was born on 3rd November 1933 in Santiniketan, West Bengal, the University town established by Rabindranath Tagore. Sen hails from a well-known liberal academic family. Sen's father was Ashutosh Sen and his mother was Amita Sen. Sen began his high-school education at St Gregory's School in Dhaka in 1941, in modern-day Bangladesh. His family migrated to India following partition in 1947. Sen studied at the Visva-Bharati University School and Presidency College, Kolkata before moving to Trinity College, Cambridge, where he earned a First Class BA (Honours) in 1956 and then a Ph.D. in 1959. At the age of 23 Sen became Professor and Head of Department of Economics at Jadavpur University, Kolkata. Sen won a Prize Fellowship at Trinity College and he took the radical decision of studying philosophy. That proved to be of immense help to his later research. Royal Swedish academy conferred the Nobel Prize to Sen in 1988.

Metaphysics and Epistemology

For Sen, Reality is that which we see through our senses and understand through our intellect. Human beings have the ability to treat themselves as subject and everything else as object. The subject finds himself as a relational being, a person belongs to different groups. The same person can be Indian citizen, a British or American resident, a poet, a government employee, a man or a woman, a student of philosophy etc. All these belongings put some force over his choices and decisions that he takes and answers he gives for the problems he faces today and on his priorities. This complexity is complexity of metaphysics for him. This is very much linked with epistemology. Once we understand individual as member of a group and nature of group as multi-dimensional with sub-classifications we enter into a complex web. Here comes up clash of interests, role of ambiguity. For Sen, the central issue in epistemology is clarification of this ambiguity.

Ethics and Economics

Amartya Sen's ethics has the foundations of liberalism and welfare in it. Liberalism accepts freedom, tolerance and democracy. He appreciates the intellectual plurality of Indian heritage and says question and dissent is there in Indian blood. He proves it in his book '*The Argumentative Indian*' by quoting from ancient texts. The tolerance of minority views and criticism we can see even in scriptures like *Bhagavad Gita*. He is inspired by Gandhian ideals of economic and social welfare based on ethics. His sensitivity to the marginalised is visible in his works and attitude to economic theories of capitalism and communism. According to him the slogans like "you have to break some eggs to make an omelette" is dreadfully misleading and mistaken in terms of understanding the nature of human. Thus, he stands for participatory economics. According to him, economics without human welfare is fruitless. Thus, economist must look into grass root situations.

Poverty as Deprivation

Poverty must be defined not as deprivation of food, but in terms of illiteracy, poor health care system, inadequate land reforms, gender differences, deprivation of women and positive neglect of children. He says "with uncomfortable areas of our socio-economic life such as inequality, deprivation, sex bias, malnutrition, illness and starvation ever present, the economist has a duty to suggest measures to remove them. He has to examine the legal system and the wage structure. Our policy makers are not to be obsessed with total consumption but with the provision of basic needs for the people's needs." It is his concept of justice that forced him to go into the root causes of deprivations in society. All types of disadvantages, class division, caste division, backward region, inequalities within family in terms of schooling, food, and allocation of resources, etc., he treats. In this context, he criticizes some traditional cultural values like self-sacrificing, which disproportionately praised, idealized and idolized.

Social Philosophy

Sen's papers in the late 1960s and early 1970s helped develop the philosophy of social choice. In 1981, Sen in his book *Poverty and Famines,* demonstrated that famine occurs not only from a lack of food, but from inequalities built into mechanisms for distributing food. He presents data that there was an adequate food supply, but particular groups of people including rural landless labourers and urban service providers like haircutters did not have the monetary means to acquire food as its price rose rapidly due to factors that include military acquisition, panic buying, hoarding, and price gouging. Sen revealed that in many cases of famine, food supplies were not significantly reduced. In Bengal, for example, food production, while down on the previous year, was higher than in previous non-famine years. Sen points to a number of social and economic factors, such as declining wages, unemployment, rising food prices and poor food-distribution systems. These issues led to starvation among certain groups in society. His capabilities approach focused on positive freedom, a person's actual ability to be or do something, rather than on negative freedom approaches, which are common in economics and simply focuses on non-interference. In the Bengal famine, rural labourers' negative freedom to buy food was not affected. However, they still starved because they were not positively free to do anything; they did not have the functioning of nourishment, nor the capability to escape morbidity.

Welfare Economics

Welfare economics seeks to evaluate economic policies in terms of their effects on the well-being of the community. Sen addressed problems related to individual rights (including formulation of the liberal paradox), justice and equity, majority rule, and the availability of information about individual conditions, inspired researchers to turn their attention to issues of basic welfare. Sen devised methods of measuring poverty that yielded useful information for improving economic conditions for the poor. For instance, his theoretical work on inequality provided an explanation for why there are fewer women than men in India and China despite the fact that in the West and in poor but medically unbiased countries, women have lower mortality rates at all ages, live longer, and make a slight majority of the population. Sen claimed that this skewed ratio results from the better health treatment and childhood opportunities afforded to boys in those countries, as well as sex-specific abortion.

Capability Approach

Sen's revolutionary contribution to the philosophy of development economics and social indicators is the concept of 'capability.' He argues that governments should be measured against the concrete capabilities of their citizens. This is because top-down development will always trump human rights as long as the definition of terms remains in doubt (Is a 'right' something that must be provided or something that simply cannot be taken away?). For instance, in the United States citizens have a hypothetical 'right' to vote. To Sen, this concept is fairly empty. In order for citizens to have a capacity to vote, they first must have 'functionings.' These 'functionings' can range from the very broad, such as the availability of education, to the very specific, such as transportation to the polls. Only when such barriers are removed can the citizen truly be said to act out of personal choice. It is up to the individual society to make the list of minimum capabilities guaranteed by that society.

Sen was seen as a ground-breaker among late twentieth-century economists for his insistence on discussing issues seen as marginal by most economists. He mounted one of the few major challenges to the economic model that posited self-interest as the prime motivating factor of human activity. His work helped to re-prioritize a significant sector of economists and development workers, even the policies of the United Nations. Governments and international organizations handling food crises were influenced by Sen's work. His views encouraged policy makers to pay attention not only to alleviate immediate suffering but also to finding ways to replace the lost income of the poor, as, for example, through public-works projects, and to maintain stable prices for food. A vigorous defender of political freedom, Sen believed that famines do not occur in functioning democracies because their leaders must be more responsive to the demands of the citizens. In order for economic growth to be achieved, he argued, social reforms, such as improvements in education and public health, must precede economic reform.

4.3. E. V. R. Periyar (1879-1973)

E.V. Ramasamy is popularly known as Periyar (great soul). Periyar was a rationalist par excellence and a humanist. He stood against all exploits of humans made in the name of religion. He is rightly called as the father of Dravidian rationalism. He was born on 17 September, 1879 to Vekata Naicker and Chinna Thayammal, at Erode in Tamil Nadu. He had only a primary education and entered into his father's trade. As a boy he started questioning the contradictions and illusions in the fables of Hindu religion and rationalism and atheism blossomed in him. He left his wife and family in 1904 and traveled to Andhra and reached Kasi. In Varanasi, refusal of food from *mutt*, the immoral activities and worst ugly scenes on 'holy city' triggered his rational mind to give up his renunciation. On his return to Erode he entered into public life by rendering social services. His involvement in Tamil revivalism, freedom movement, helped him to become a fighter of social justice, rationalism and self-respect movement of Dravidians. In 1925, he found the self-respect movement after his exit from the congress party.

By his public meetings he kindled the awakening of the Dravidian race for freeing themselves from slavery enforced by Brahmins. He instituted 'self-respect marriage,' without any religious rituals or Brahmins officiating it. He encouraged inter-caste marriages and widow re-marriages. He was an inspiration and an activist for Dravidian movement, claim for separate Dravida country, anti-Hindi agitations during and post-independence period. He started journals in Tamil: *Kudiarasu* (People's government), *Puratchi* (Revolt), *Pakutharivu* (Discernment), and *Viduthalai* (Liberty). Periyar started to wear black shirt to symbolically announce the degraded situation of the Dravidians. Periyar stressed that the Dravidians are in a, "compelling need to preserve the self-respect of their race, language, and culture which had been degraded by the brahminical dominance through their caste-system and superstitions of the Hindu religion." He died on 24 December, 1973. Periyar dedicated his life and activities to devote service to spread secularism, humanism and rationalism. He has been known for fierce ideological battles he fought and won for social justice, gender justice and for upholding human rights.

Secular Humanism

His famous declaration, 'forget God; think of humans,' is the gist of secular humanism envisaged under the constitution. He with a prophetic vision and foresight made this famous declaration to forget God and think of humans. He said 'man-made religion and God' have outlived their usefulness and it has helped only commercialization and exploitation of people in the name of religion. As religion instead of being a cohesive force has now become a destructive divisive force and has under-mined the values of humanism, love and tolerance to fellow human beings with compassion, piety to promote human progress and prosperity. His historical battle at Vaikom for upholding the human rights of untouchables for right of entry into temple was hallmark of his achievements. He propagated humanism as one of tenets of his self-respect movement. His secularism and humanism were based on a rationalist philosophy motivated by compassion and piety for fellow human beings. His humanism affirms the dignity of each individual and advocated participatory democracy reflecting the sovereign will of the people to work for preservation and promotion of human rights and implementation of social justice. His humanist approach responds only to social ethics and morals and not to religious dogmas, with the sole aim to promote human progress and prosperity.

Rationalism of Periyar

Everyone has to develop scientific temper and spirit of inquiry and this is precisely the basis of rationalism propagated by Periyar. As a social leader, he preached rationalism as a creed to be followed in day to day life. Periyar realized that the presence of many irrational beliefs and superstition is the result of not developing the spirit of inquiry. The tendency of people to easily believe without questioning the divine powers claimed by fake 'god-men' and other super natural events are the result of not developing rational spirit of inquiry. For Periyar, rationalism is a mental attitude that unreservedly accepts the supremacy of reason and aims at systems of thought verifiable by experience and independent of all arbitrary assumptions or authority.

Rationalism provides an alternative way of life and philosophy for those who desire to throw away the orthodox religion and morals based on fear of God. Its main objective is to liberate human thought from the limitations of caste, creed, religion and nationality and promote an attitude of optimism to develop healthy and dynamic minds. Rationalism according to him, is, "the critical analysis of all things pertaining to the functioning of the human mind and not take anything for granted. Rationalism is not just atheism but the questioning of assumptions and certainties that had been handed down to us from ages past." Rationalism is the triumph of reason in human affairs, in the life of the individuals and in the society. It affirms that humanity is one and indivisible and inculcates the spirit of tolerance and promotes universal brotherhood. Rationalism aims at the good of the community, by forging unity and promoting humanism and makes them work for social welfare and for the good of humankind.

His rationalism is against the stagnant static existence of people shackled by age-old irrational traditional beliefs and practices and helped people to lead a dynamic life guided by reason and humanism. The basic principle is not to believe anything without questioning, not to be narrow-minded and dogmatic, but to be liberal and tolerant in their views. Unlike others, Periyar carried the message of rationalism and humanism to the people and delivered it in a language understood and well received by the illiterate masses. It brought about an awakening among the people and made them think for themselves.

Egalitarian Society

As a social reformer, he was vehemently against casteism. He understood that casteism is the main impediment to unity and progress and firmly believed that social uplift is possible only when it is eradicated. For him, social justice will remain a distant dream if social order based on equality of status and equality of opportunity to all, is not brought out. His self-respect movement has strived hard to evolve a casteless society where caste will not determine the social status and the rights of the persons and act as a barrier for man's progress. His anti-brahminism was an attempt to level the society and lay the foundation for permanent casteless society.

His tireless strenuous efforts and a massive attempt to educate the masses for a casteless egalitarian society through his speeches, writings and his own conduct, left behind a society more alert, more questioning, less gullible and more rationalist in outlook. Periyar was a crusader for social reforms by ceaseless propaganda molded a new social order and paved the way for a casteless society of equals with secularism and rationalism as the basis and how he brought about a great social revolution and reformation without violence, bloodshed and loss of human life, the vision and dream of poets of winning war without arms.

Anti-brahminism

Periyar's chief agenda was to democratize the Dravidian society. When he saw that Brahminism was the chief opposing force which hindered him to achieve his goal, Periyar turned against Brahminism by using atheism and rationalism as his two cardinal weapons. Periyar exposed the false religiosity of the Brahmins. Periyar said, "The Brahmins are making you fools in the name of God. They make you have faith in superstitions. They lead a very comfortable life while condemning you as untouchable. They bargain with you to offer prayers to God on your behalf. I strongly condemn this brokerage business and warn you not to believe such Brahmins anymore." As a polemic against Brahminism Periyar developed atheism. His boldly asserted, "There is no God. There is no God at all. He who created God is a fool. He who propagates God is a rogue. He who worships God is a barbarian." Periyar questioned the mythologies and superstitious beliefs from a relatively young age.

Dravidian Self-Respect Movement

The Self-Respect Movement initiated by Periyar stood against "Brahmin supremacy and domination of certain castes in the name of religion... It demanded the abandonment of caste bigotry and intellectual arrogance". It was a rationalist movement launched, "to liberate people from theological thinking and to secure for all people equality in life irrespective of sex and status." The entire agenda of the Self-Respect Movement rested on five pillars: "(1) No God, (2) No Religion, (3) No Gandhi, (4) No Congress, and (5) No Brahmins." When Periyar held the first Self-Respect Provincial Conference at Chengalpet, several resolutions such as, "eradication of untouchability, encouraging of inter-caste marriages, boycott of *purohits* (priests), dropping of caste suffixes to personal names, ensuring equality to women with property rights, widow remarriage, etc., were passed." Periyar's Self-respect Movement was without doubt a barricade for the Hindutva ideologies and a barrier for the vested interest of the Brahmins. The downtrodden were highly guided and enlightened by the various speeches Periyar and his associates delivered. In south India, we can say that Periyar literally brought self-awareness and self-respect among the then subjugated masses. He taught self-esteem and helped millions to come out of their inferiority complex and slave mentalities infused for centuries by the Brahmin overlords.

Atheism as Critique of Religion

In the eyes of the general public, Periyar is seen as an avowed atheist. Though Periyar was an atheist, promoting atheism was not his principal task. Periyar was motivated by a reconstructive vision. He wanted to rouse the Dravidian society from its dogmatic slumber and cleanse their minds from the incredulity perpetuated by Brahminism. Periyar was much critical of the notion of God. He says, "of all the foolish notions which ruined the human race on earth, it is the thought of God that is of foremost significance." He was too bold for his day when he declared that 'god' is a myth. For the followers of Periyar, to believe in God is, "to believe in irrational beings who exercise autocratic powers over the destiny of man and the world of nature." Periyar feels that the concept of God is in itself humanity's projection of its own desired self-perfection. God is seen as perfect or privileged 'Human.' So humans see their God in anthropomorphic expressions. The God of a particular people reflects their particular characteristics. His objective in promoting atheism was not to make an anti-God society. He aimed more on the, "reformation of religion from its superstitious and irrational divine elements. The society in which he lived makes it clear why Periyar did not accept God. We can say "if he accepted God, he had to accept Hindu religion. If he accepted Hindu religion, he had to naturally accept the tie, i.e., *Varnasrama Dharma*, the high and low birth etc. So as a rationalist, Periyar was not prepared to compromise even a bit with the God or Godhead."

Social Justice and Women Empowerment

When there was no constitutional mandate for implementing social justice, Periyar took up battle for it by his Self-respect movement to remove social inequalities. Equality of opportunities to all, was met with by Periyar propagating the implementation of the communal Government Order (G.O) that gave representation to all communities in Government service proportionate to their population. When that G.O was struck down by courts as unconstitutional Periyar's agitation led to the constitutional amendment under Articles 15 (4) ensuring reservation to backward classes in educational institutions and Government Service thus ensuring equality of opportunity. He originated the battle for gender justice, when there was no constitutional mandate guaranteeing equality of sexes and prohibiting discrimination based on Sex. He advocated women's right to divorce their husbands and remarry, the virtue of chastity as not being a one-way traffic must be equally enforced both for men and women, the freedom of choice to conceive and bear children must be given to women, and women should have equal rights of inheritance like men in the properties of their parents and their deceased husband, the right of widow for remarriage and restraint on child marriage.

Chapter 5

SUBALTERN THINKERS

New quest for social reform came from people who had experienced more bitterly the inequalities and injustices of the Indian social system. Modern India heralded a new age of growing subaltern assertion, from Dalits, Tribals and Women. For want of space we focus only on Dalit thinkers here. Subalterns are those people who are marginalized, oppressed and separated from the society's established welfare. They have been discriminated against socially, religiously, politically, economically, and above all, ideologically. They are treated as polluted people destined to live in humiliation, pain and constant suffering. Subaltern philosophy is relatively a contemporary branch of philosophy emerging from the philosophizing of the 'wounded psyche'. It arises from the cries, sufferings and struggle of the oppressed. This philosophy is the war cry of the oppressed raised against the oppressing social structure of the Indian society.

Subaltern thinkers have envisioned egalitarian society without discrimination and subjugation. From the ancient times, there had been strong voices and ideological systems that challenged the discriminative and oppressive structures and ideologies of Brahmanical hegemony. Buddhism and Jainism, Bhakti Movements and Protest Movements, the Mass Conversion Movements towards Islam, Christianity, and Buddhism, and the Counter-Cultural Movements initiated by Mahatma Phule, Iyothee Thass, Ambedkar, Narayana Guru, and many other contemporary intellectuals stand the test of time for upholding a profound social philosophy of the Dalits. We pick up some prominent Dalit personalities who voiced such reformative measures and are not generally given much attention in Indian modern philosophical discussions. We rightly capture the continual struggle of the Dalits in the ideology and activism of the contemporary Dalit thinkers.

5.1. Ambedkar (1891-1956)

Dr. B.R. Ambedkar, was one of the most learned among the political and social leaders of the 20th century in India. He wrote many books and edited many papers. He wrote not only on the problems of the Dalits, but also on economics, politics, religion, minorities, education, labour, stratification of society etc. Ambedkar was born on April 14, 1891 in a low caste family of suppressed *Mahar* community of Mhow in Madhya Pradesh. After his graduation, he received scholarship from the king of Baroda for higher studies in USA and England. He graduated in law and took a doctorate in economics. He returned to Bombay to practice law. On 14th October 1935, he declared that he would not die in Hinduism. Ambedkar is regarded as the chief architect of the Constitution of India as he served the country as the chairman of the Constitution Drafting Committee. On August 15, 1947, he was made the minister of law in the Central Cabinet and he resigned that post in 1951 due to the difference of opinion on the bill on Hindu code. He embraced neo-Buddhism with his three lakh followers on October 14, 1956 just before his death on December 6, 1956. His works include: *Slavery and Untouchability; Which is Worse?; Annihilation of Caste; A Reply to Mahatma Gandhi; What Congress and Gandhi Have Done to Untouchables?; Who Were Shudras?; The Buddha and his Dhamma; Annihilation of Caste.*

Critique of Caste System

For Ambedkar, social reform is absolutely essential and prior to any political revolution. Ambedkar systematically evolved a thorough criticism against *Chaturvarnyam*. It cannot be a basis for society, but liberty, equality and fraternity as basis. Caste system is basically unjust, which is to be rejected. Gandhi accepts the idea of *varna* as hereditary transmission of social function. Arya samaj rejected the idea of caste based on birth and speak of caste based on natural aptitudes. Ambedkar rejects this approach as impracticable, harmful and as a whole a miserable failure. It is the determination and division of four castes on the basis of *varna* or colour. His attack upon caste system was not an outburst but principle based. "To me this *Chaturvarnya* with its old labels is utterly repellent and my whole being rebels against it. But, I do not wish to rest my objection to *Chaturvarnya* on mere grounds of sentiments. There are more solid grounds on which I rely for my opposition to it." He found caste system as out dated, impracticable, irrational and superstitious social practice. He narrated the damages done by it on the society, "Caste has killed public spirit. Caste has destroyed the sense of public charity. Caste has made public opinion impossible. Virtue has become caste ridden and morality has become caste bound. There is no sympathy to the deserving. There is no appreciation of the meritorious." For the decay of a society are not these evils enough? He fought consistently for human dignity and social equality. Ambedkar's prime concern was the establishment of an egalitarian society. He set annihilation of caste as his goal. He believed that the real independence of India was possible only by it. He claimed that social progress and stability were possible in an equitable society.

Annihilation of Caste System

Annihilation of casteism is one of the most essential elements in Ambedker's socio-philosophical frame. It cannot be done just by abolishing the sub-sects, nor by inter caste dining. Ambedkar proposes a solution on two levels: (a) the proximate, immediate means to remove caste is intermarriage. (b) But, the fundamental remedy consists in bringing about a social reform before political reforms and in denying the faith in *śāstras*, where he says; "you must not only discard the *śāstras*, you must deny their authority. You must have the courage to tell the Hindus what is more wrong with their religion." According to him the Hindu is the sick man/woman of the society who makes other people also sick. His protest against Hinduism was expressed by burning *Manusmṛti* in a public meeting.

The ideal society is based on liberty, equality and fraternity. Liberty includes the fundamental physical liberty and liberty of movement. It includes also economic liberty to earn and possess. It includes the social liberty to decide one's own profession freely. Equality: many forms of inequalities in human existence; equality is an equality of rights. Fraternity: it does not refer to a moral law of charity but to the rule of social endosmosis. This would lead to social democracy.

Religious Thoughts

He gives an atheistic interpretation of the message of Buddha. He rejects the idea of super natural causes as going against man's freedom. Law of *kamma* or causation is all inclusive; all events can be explained in terms of a given cause in this world. These causes can be known by man's reason. Once more there is no place for a God who would be beyond *kamma*. Buddhism is rationalism for him. Ambedkar's atheism is further expressed when he considers belief in God as 'non-*dhamma*'.

According to him, Buddhism rejects the idea of the human soul. The idea of soul can be rejected since no one has ever seen the soul. We find in man a physical element and an element of consciousness. This is sufficient to explain man completely. Having done away with the soul, Ambedkar tries to preserve the theory of rebirth. The theory is reduced to a purely scientific theory on conservation of energy. What happens when the body dies? The body ceases to produce energy. But this is only a part of the answer. Because death also means that whatever energy that has escaped from the body joins the general mass of energy playing about in the universe. Annihilation has therefore a twofold aspect. In one of its aspects it means cessation of production of energy. In another aspect it means a new addition to the stock of general floating mass of energy.

Having rejected the idea of God and of the soul, he still accepts that religion is very basic to society. But, religion becomes a purely moral religion. Religion is not a morality based on God but a morality based on the universal law of *kamma*. That is on the basic idea that the effect of the deed is bound to follow the deed. Concretely man must follow his *dhamma*, so as to help in building the kingdom of righteousness. Man follows his *dhamma* in trying to place at the center of his life the following; purity and detachment: purity in thought, words, deeds and complete detachment from craving and from all desires. Insight: (*prajña*) the brahmanic ideal of *jñāna* is here replaced by the idea of insight which is control over one's consciousness and capacity to apply one's conscious effect to good. Virtue (*sīla*): while insight refers to proper thinking, *sīla* refers to proper action. Universal love (*kāruna*): contains the two basic attitudes of *kāruna* and love for all men and *maitri* which is love for everything that exists.

Political Thoughts

His political thinking seems to revolve around the following two convictions: (a) Rights are protected not by laws, but by the social and moral conscience of the society. (b) A democratic form of government presupposes a democratic form of society. Indian constitution remains indebted to Ambedkar for his significant contribution to the peaceful living in the land of diversity. For Ambedkar, state is to provide security against internal disorder and external aggression. The state stands for the welfare of its members. It is the people who make the state and hence the state is to serve the needs of the people. It is a means to achieve the common good of the society. Between state and society, Ambedkar would prefer society as the primary and state as secondary. State, according to Ambedkar, is not of a divine origination but of human origination. To him, the state is a human organization with its objective being the protection of the rights of the individuals. One of his major convictions evident in his political philosophy can be stated as. The state was not an end in itself, but only means for the furtherance of human ends in the interests of a better future of the society. He greatly emphasized the role of the law of the state in the growth of the individual. To him, law was an important factor in maintaining social peace and justice among different groups of people. Thus, he concludes that all are equal before the law. He upheld right as the basis for the human development and the nation at large.

Dr. B.R. Ambedkar's social, political and economic thoughts, religious convictions and political strategies for the liberation of the weakest in the society have huge impact during and after Independence movement. His social criticism was a demand for social justice. He felt the religious reformation and political movements of his time sidelined the social and economic exploitation in the name of caste. Thus he started with independent movement and action program for the liberation of the depressed classes. Organizing the depressed classes and seprating them from Hindu fold would be a workable strategy to liberate them. Otherwise, they would be assimilated into Hinduism without getting liberation from caste oppression. He was attracted to Buddhist humanism, compassion, love and selfless collective living. He made use of political position and space available to him for providing provisions for liberation of depressed classes and women.

5.2. Mahatma Phule (1827-1890)

Known as Mahatma Jyotirao Phule was an activist, thinker, social reformer, philosopher and a revolutionary. His main interests were on ethics, religion and humanism. He was the pioneer of women's education in Maharashtra. He is one of the most important figures in social reform movement in Maharashtra and is rightly called as the father of Indian social revolution. Phule was born in a Mali family in a caste perceived to be inferior caste by certain sections of the society. From his experience of being insulted by family members of his Brahmin friend he faced the divide created by the caste system. He developed the sense of social justice becoming passionately critical of casteism. He firmly believed in education as of vital importance in addressing social inequalities. His influence and remarkable contribution towards education, eradication of caste, empowerment of women and widow upliftment and removal of untouchability are commendable. He is a well-known reformist for his efforts to educate women and Dalits. Phule advocated a perspective from *Sudra* and *Adiśudra* social location situated in the duty soil where they toil and moil against high class or Brahminical perspective to preserve their domination, promoted by the writers of his time who very much influenced the British Government.

Human Freedom

For Phule, freedom is very essential for human beings. "When man is free, he can clearly convey his thoughts to people through writing or speech. But, if he does not have freedom, then he is unable to communicate his thoughts, however, beneficial they might be to the others, and consequently, they just evaporate into thin air." A free man will never hesitate to claim his rights which are granted by God to all humans. He rests happy only when he gets his rights back.

Satya Shodhak Samaj

He formed a Society of Seekers of Truth, *Satya Shodhak Samaj* with the objective of organizing masses to liberate the Dalits and to prevent them from exploitations and atrocities done by the dominating castes. He believed in and propagated education to attain equal rights for peasants and lower castes. The main objective of his Samaj was to prevent people's exploitation by the upper caste like Brahmans. Through the *Samaj* he refused to regard the Vedas as *sacrosanct.* He opposed idolatry and denounced thoroughly caste system. He wanted to create a new social system based on freedom, equality, brotherhood, human dignity, economic justice and value devoid of exploitation.

He wished that the present society over throw the old, unequal and exploitative social system and the values based on it. He attacked blind faith and the faith in the exploitative and oppressive religious books that come up with dominating people in name of gods. His samaj propounded the spread of rational thinking and rejected the need for a Brahman priestly class as educational and religious leaders. With help of Shahu Maharaj, the king of Kolhapur the Samaj spread to the remotest parts of Maharashtra. It carried on the work of removal of superstition vigorously. Phule tore to pieces the misleading myths from the minds of people. He showed people that yielding to fate, astrology and other such rituals and God-men are irrational and absurd.

According to Phule, "God is Creator, Governor, and Protector and who himself is all Holiness." But, Manu and others of his class have distorted the idea of God by attributing the most immoral, inhuman, unjust actions and deeds to the Supreme Being. From this idea of God emerged a social order that dehumanizes the Śudras and the Adiśudras. They were exploited at all levels. The Brahmins under the guise of religion control all spheres of life of Sudras. He tried to remove the factors that breed blind faith. The religious texts and activities are to be tested with rationalism. He characterized blind faith as outwardly religious but in essence politically motivated. He accused them of upholding the teachings of religion and refusing to be rational. At the root of all calamities, maintains Phule has a blind faith in religious books that are said to be created or inspired by God.

5.3. Iyothee Thass (1845-1914)

Iyothee Thass was born on 20th May 1845. His original name was Kathavarayan. After obtaining expertise of Siddha medicine from his guru Iyothee Doss Kaviraja Pandithar he called himself as Iyothee Doss after his guru. He was well-versed in Tamil, Pali, Sanskrit and English languages. He established Advaitanta Sabha at Nilgiris in 1870 and Dravida Mahajana Sabha in 1891 and established Sakiya Bouddharkal Sangam. We find in Advaitananda Sabha his objective was to organize the downtrodden. A search for a paradigm shift was found in Thass' transition from Advaita to Buddhism. By 1890, he preferred to revive Tamil Buddhism, giving an identity to subalterns and constructing a collective consciousness; a construction indeed for their empowerment. Thass had preferential concern towards the children of the marginalized and established educational institutions for them at Chennai.

On 19th June, 1907 he started a weekly known as "*Oru Paisa Thamizhan.*" Essays in *Tamizhan* were published establishing Tamil classics like *Manimēkalai* and ethical works like *Tirukkural* and *Atticcuvati* as Buddhist works. Thass' *Puttaratu Ādhivēdam* is his *magnum opus,* written in 1912, to explain Buddhism to new converts. The book based on Tamil and Pāli works is a standing testimony to his scholarship and erudition. It narrates Buddha's history and Buddhist religious doctrines. *Buddhist Doctrines – Question and Answers,* 1912, had been published several times. *Indirar Desa charithiram* 1931 narrates a new history that India came to be known as Bharat even before the advent of the Aryans and Buddhism was the religion of the rulers of this country. Avvaiyar and her *Atticcuti, konṛaivēntan and vetri ñānam* are interpreted in a new light. *Vivāka Villakkam* 1926, tells what the reformed marriage procedure was. Denial of rights to widows and unwanted marriage rituals are condemned. *Harichandran Lies* 1931, special *sangai thelivu, yathārtha Brāhmana* and *vēsha Brāhmana – vetānta* details, *Nandan* History *Trick* – all these contain Buddha's preaching in Tamil and Pāli.

Buddhism as Subaltern Movement

Iyothee Thass made strenuous efforts in constructing a collective consciousness for the subalterns as '*pūrva* Buddhist' and as original Tamils. Tamil Buddhism of Thass remained a construct, conceptual framework, like that of 'Hindu' or 'Tamil Saiva' constructs. After Thass, there were no takers for this conceptual framework. Although Tamil Buddhism failed to become a strong mass movement, Thass' contribution is praiseworthy for he had powerfully and forcefully argued for constructing a consciousness for the subalterns.

Certainly it initiates a lively discussion of consciousness, individual or collective identity, as contested and constructed reality, not as a given or naturally emerging one. Giving the oppressed people a religious identity, he affirms that religion becomes an ideology, socially determined and as culturally constructed phenomenon. Having understood that religious symbols are influential and authoritative, he tried to create new worlds of symbols and their meaning, worldviews and ideologies. The construction of different worldview and religious identity happen in concrete living situations. In subaltern awareness it is the unjust, inhuman and oppressive caste structure that stimulates the aspiration for constructing distinctive identity. Necessity of self-assertion and self-determination is very much felt. For him, Emancipation is not in just socio-political field but in affirmation of the collective self.

Revivalism of Buddhism has played a vital role in emergence of Subaltern consciousness. There was always a connection between these, as Buddhism was taken as an adequate challenging tradition to the caste-ridden tradition. Consciousness of oppression and freedom from oppression was sought by having recourse to reviving Buddhism. As dominance was equated with Vedism, Buddhism was sought after for emancipation. As a counter movement, Buddhism was seen as the pointer, inspirer and action oriented philosophy.

Thass' choice of Buddhism even before Ambedkar, was to create a counter culture against revivalist tradition of the time. Indeed, it was a paradigm for critiquing the metaphysical frame work of traditional thinking. Buddhism was seen as a critique of oppressed caste hierarchy. In search for a specific identity, the subalterns tried to take recourse to Buddhism. In an era of awareness of liberty, equality and human dignity, Tamil Buddhist movement strove hard to give distinctive identity, to create collective consciousness of their oppressed state and to enable self-esteem. Later for Ambedkar Buddhism proposes a social reconstruction for alleviating suffering of the oppressed. Embracing Buddhism is not for its fighting nature, but as an ideological revolution, a counter culture and ethics. For speaking out the suffering and social injustice and for rising against them for the liberation of the people, subaltern thinkers took up Buddhism as a cultural weapon for Dalit struggle for identity.

Subaltern Religion

Against the practice of exclusion by the dominant caste groups, he promoted idea of inclusion and pleaded for democratization of traditional religion. He said: "We have heard that God and temples are common for all castes of the world. If that is so, why people of this community following Vaishnava or Saivaite tradition cannot be allowed to enter Vishnu or Shiv temples? By allowing them, won't they prosper through mutual love and the religions also be strengthened?" While critically analyzing the texts on God and soul, Iyothee Thass came up with a new discourse on God. The term God refers to those men and women, who through their own morally right conduct towards their fellow human beings and society have become immortalized in history and inspiration for subsequent generations. God is an ideal term and invitation to all similarly raise themselves morally to the status of the Divine. Veneration of these gods is neither out of fear nor for favor but a celebratory remembrance to strengthen one's own resolve to become like them. He highlighted the differences between Sankritic-Shasthraic Brahminism and Sramanism-Buddhism. Brahminical religion introduced a hierarchical society in the form of caste system. Caste system elevated Brahmins to the level of gods and divided the society into upper classes and lower classes and treated women as inferior groups. A righteous life taught by Buddha is religion for him. He tried to unmask the distorted meanings of religious beliefs and practices and reinterpreted and reconstructed the past in the course of self-affirmation and erected a new sacred universe.

Buddhist Ideals for Living

According to Thass, the three fundamental ethical teachings of Buddha are: Don't sin (*Kanma Bhāgai*); Do good (*Artha Bhāgai*); Purify your heart (*Gnana Bhāgai*). These fundamental teachings are further explicated in the four (*Bhēdas*): *Aram, Poruḷ, Inbam, Vēdu*. Each *Bhāgai* has got eight deeper understandings which are called *upanidam*. Apart from three *Bhāgai*, the fourth one is called *Niruvāna Bhāgai* which emphasizes renunciation. He mentions about *Devanilai*, which means completely removing the evil desires and deeds in oneself, engulfed in virtues of compassion, love and forbearance and loving relationship with all creatures. Those people who have obtained the status of *Devanilai* are called Devars. The Buddha was the *Ādidēvan* and *Ādināthan*.

Towards Inclusive Society

"Consciousness of oppression" is an uneasy, disturbing consciousness. It is an urge, a will to change the so far held normative and structural social relations. As praxis oriented consciousness of oppression in all socio-political, religious spheres, it is a strong aspiration to challenge and change the strong normative and structural social relations. The rise of consciousness of oppression is "process by which the different individuals and groups become conscious" The nationalist surge was seen as reassertion of the hierarchical ideology. While Dravidian movements and Tamil Saiva movement raised voice against Brahmanism, they did not touch the basic caste structure. But for Thass, shattering the caste structure is basic for giving an identity for the subalterns. To constructing an identity other than Brahmin/non-brahmin, Thass preferred Buddhism.

Iyothee Thass remains the first recognized anti-Brahmin leader of the Madras Presidency. He was also the first notable Dalit leader to embrace Buddhism. Iyothee Thass influenced the Dravidian consciousness, rationalist movement, self-respect movement in Tamil Nadu. Thass, after epistemologically and historically deconstructed the current status of Dalits, he took ethical steps to regain their lost subjectivity. Revivalism of Buddhism has played a vital role in emergence of Subaltern consciousness. It was transformatory or emancipatory movement for the subalterns. Dalit Emancipation was his focus and he established a genuine history and respect for Dalits.

5.4. Narayana Guru (1856-1928)

Narayana Guru was a Dalit thinker, spiritual leader, social reformer and a sage in the modern period of India. He was born in Ezhava family at

Chempazhanthy, near Trivandrum. His father Madan Asan was a great scholar in Sanskrit, Medicine and Astrology and he was Narayan Guru's first teacher. Later, he was sent to a gurukulam. He was married to Kaligamma and later he left his wife, his people and his village. He started on his solitary pursuit in search of meaning of life. Born as Ezhava which was a caste considered in between the upper and lowest strata in the caste hierarchy, he and his society suffered social injustice. The Guru's literary works are in Malayalam, Sanskrit, Tamil languages, and these works are of a conceptual and aesthetic quality at par with the upanishads.

He revolted against casteism and reformed the society by rejecting caste divisions in the society. When he consecrated an idol, he remarked that it was not a Brahmin Siva but an Ezhava Siva. God is neither a priest nor a peasant. He is in all. He is all. The news of this silent but daring revolution echoed throughout the far flung frontiers of India. He walked on foot to almost every village in Kerala. In Sivagiri, he established his center. In 1913, temple-entry was banned to the low caste, he launched a counter movement involving common people and this made a lasting imprint on the contemporary, religious and political renaissance of India. Later his values of social revolution ultimately achieved the desired effect of throwing open temples to all castes.

He founded in 1903, Sri Narayana Dharma Paripalana Yogam for uplift of the lower classes of the society. Hundreds of institutions embodying his principles sprang up throughout Kerala. His purpose was to lay the foundation for a co-operative brotherhood which, through spontaneous public service, would truly reflect the long-cherished unity at all levels.

Revolutionary Advaita

He used the Advaita Vedanta as a tool for transforming the society. Guru's philosophy, which is fundamentally of Advaitic and non-dual wisdom in principles, further extended advaita concepts into practical modes of self-realization through spiritual education, compassion and vision for peaceful co-existence of the human race, whilst promoting social equality and universal brotherhood. His philosophy of non-violence and *ahimsa* strongly denounced discrimination in the name of caste or religion, and emphasized focusing on education and private enterprise for the ongoing uplift of the quality of life. The aim of the reformer was the abolition of untouchability. He removed the outer layer of meaningless *varna* and brought to light the inner core of a common *dharma.* He established that belief in *varna* and *jāti* only denies the fundamental doctrine of non-duality and allows elements that destroy the unification and integration of the human race.

Concept of God and Self

Guru's philosophical thought is that it reveals to man his own divinity, his essential oneness with God and his capacity and competence to realize his own identity. Guru stressed the non-duality of the ultimate reality. The supreme is immortal, which has been designated as that which has no origin or dissolution. God is one and not mentioned by any name. The eight qualities of God mentioned by Guru in his poem *daiva dāsakam,* are omniscience, omnipotence, omnipresence, self-dependence, purity, truth, grace and full of love. Through several steps, man will realize his high destination, *ātman* the absolute. He will first worship God as one outside of himself, then as the whole of which he is a part; and lastly as one without a second, his own real self. Without this self, nothing can exist or be known or be experienced. Just as all rivers flow in to the ocean, the individual souls will finally merge in Brahman. When they realize the truth, the knots of ignorance break. By denying the apparent self, one realizes the real self. The knowledge of the relationship between the adorer and the adored ultimately leads to oneness.

Concept of the World

Guru says in *darśanamāla* that mind is the cause of the perceptible world. The perceptible world is seen as a projection of His will and it has no reality. The world, the Absolute partially projected is limited manifested. Guru compares the phenomenal world in the *advaita dīpika,* to a cloth woven of superfine filaments of time and space, wherein the threads as such disappear when we view the fabric as cloth. He says that all our assumptions in the phenomenal world and the transactions that lead us to exaltations or vexations, are but mere sound and fury without any reality attached to them. Guru states that if the reality of the phenomenal world is affirmed then it is existential and if it is denied, it is substantial. As both the knower and the known have existential validity, it can be concluded that what is seen as the Reality is the effect of the one supreme eternal existence. Guru says that the wise man in his wakeful state sees this world as unreal like the silvery shade in the oyster shell, usually mistaken for silver. Guru further explains in his *brahmavidya pañchakam,* and *advaita dīpika* that the world is a mirage.

One Caste and One Religion

The specific contribution of Guru to the Advaita philosophy and religion is the theory of 'one caste, one religion and one God,' for the humanity. Humanity is the caste of human beings. His philosophy is based on his triple principle of One Caste, One Religion and One God for man. All belong to same castes; the unity is due to the fact that all have been created alike; all are of the same species. There is no difference between man and man, there is no reason why they should not eat together and inter-marry. Oneness of religion is based on the fact that all religions agree in spirit in the most essential teaching. All have a common goal; why should they fight for their faith. Religious divisions are due to the fact that each one tries to see things from his angel and fail to see the basic unity that is there beyond all these views.

Guru's concept of one God deriving from the non-dual knowledge of Brahman is the corner stone of the resulting concepts of one religion and one caste. According to him, caste is an anomaly in religion. He says that 'everyone is born as Sudra but becomes a Brahmin by his cultural action' to be accepted as valid. Further, a close examination of vedāntic texts reveals the invalidity of the caste system. All are therefore of the same caste. Thus, by advaitic reasoning, vedic authority and historical facts, Guru proclaimed the theory of one caste, one religion and one God, for mankind. The oneness of god is more an expression of advaitic monism than an expression of monotheism. This oneness has to be understood in the light of the general teaching of him. He was the essence of Vedānta or Vedanta personified. Guru re-established the advaitic philosophy so that its principles could be put into practice in the day-to-day life in a casteless but theistic society based on brotherhood and cooperative social action for achieving a better way of living.

Guru did not mention any particular religion by his idea of one religion. By one religion he means that all beings at all times, everywhere are exerting themselves to obtain happiness. This quest for happiness is the one religion in the world of which no one has any dispute. 'Whatever be his religion man must be good.' He made genuine efforts to establish spiritual unity of world religions. He wanted the world of the human race to be one solid spiritual and divine unity based on universal humanity. One religion is the common designation including all religions that advocate the ultimate good of spiritual happiness. Guru never entertained any thought of rivalry with any religion. He was of the view that no religion can conquer another religion. His teaching was that one should endeavor to be a good man whatever is his religion. He believed that the religion of the people is certainly greater than the wishes, convictions and dreams of a single individual therein. At the level of experience, all religions are one in a mystic union.

Narayana Guru was an erudite thinker who searched for not only his mental happiness but also the means of illuminating other's life. His philosophical enquiry led him to the knowledge of the 'oneness of humanity' as much as it did to the realization of the ultimate reality. His new insights into the advaitic thought gave a new light and warmth into a new world of peace, love and brotherhood and ultimately into God-hood based the realization of oneness with all humanity. Guru relentlessly fought against orthodoxy and obscurantism, untouchability and oppression, casteism and communalism and strove to establish a casteless and classless society based on love, universal brotherhood and harmony.

Chapter 6

ACADEMIC PHILOSOPHERS

Introduction of English education to form efficient civil servants in British administration was helpful in the establishing universities that catered also for philosophical reflections. Especially in Calcutta and Madras universities, there were Indian academic professors committed themselves in search and interpretation of philosophical traditions. In post-Independence period many departments of philosophy across the country sustained the reflective tradition through their dedicated thinkers. Most of them were apologetic in character falling back to ancient and classical Indian philosophical traditions to defend their intellectual heritage as to present its richness either in line with or in contrast with the Western systems. Rarely do we find original systems evolving from these philosophers. Several forums and associations kept up the spirit of enquiry and research in contemporary India. We take two representative thinkers during colonial and post-colonial periods and then give a summary of teachings of few other academic philosophers.

6.1. S. Radhakrishnan (1888-1975)

Sarvepalli Radhakrishnan was born at Tirutani in Tamil Nadu. His early years were spent in Tirutani and Tirupati. His primary education was at Primary Board High School at Tirutani and then at Lutheran Mission School at Tirupati. He joined the Voorhee's College in Vellore but switched to the Madras Christian College at the age of 17. He graduated with a Master's degree in Philosophy from the Madras Christian College in 1906. Radhakrishnan wrote his thesis for the M.A. degree on "The Ethics of the Vedanta and its Metaphysical Presuppositions". This got published as a book when he was only 20. His main works include: *East and West, Eastern Religion and Western Thought, East and West in Religion, The Reign of Religion in the Contemporary Philosophy,*

Religion and Society, The Recovery of Faith, Indian Philosophy, An Idealist View of Life, The Hindu View of Life etc.

Radhakrishnan was not a follower of any one system of thought, but open to various viewpoints presented by different philosophers. Among all the viewpoints, of course, he was more at home with the metaphysics, epistemology and ethics of Advaita Vedanta which became his line of thinking. Like Vedanta he believes that the reality is one, like Absolute Idealism, he shows that everything is a necessary aspect of the One.

Metaphysics

Following Sankara, Radhakrishnan was of the opinion that reality is Brahman that is one, spiritual, transcendent and absolute. Brahman is indescribable and manifests itself as God who is the creator of the world. The absolute is conceived by Radhakrishnan as 'Pure Consciousness', 'Pure Freedom', and Infinite Possibility.' According to Radhakrishnan, the Absolute has to be spiritual. It is conceived as a free spirit. It is free in such a way that there is nothing to limit it. Its freedom is uninterrupted. The absolute is also infinite. It is self-grounded and is the foundation of everything else. Since it is infinite it is changeless. It is also self-existent and complete-in-itself. It is also eternal in the sense of being timeless. Radhakrishnan calls the Absolute 'the whole of perfection'. Because of these reasons he asserts that the Absolute is beyond all kinds of expression.

Radhakrishnan distinguishes between the Absolute and God. He feels that in order to explain the universe it is necessary to think of a principle that would account for the order and purpose of the universe. He also feels that there has to be a principle, a God-a non-temporal and actual being-by which the indeterminateness of creativity can be transmitted into a determinate principle. So it implies that the Divine Intelligence-the creative power-has to be conceived as the intermediary between the Absolute Being and the cosmic process. It is here that the principle of God appears in the philosophy of Radhakrishnan. The supreme has been conceived as revealing itself in two ways; Absolute and Ishwara. God is the Absolute in action; it is God, the creator. The real in relation to itself is the Absolute and the real in relation to the creation is God. He believes that the Absolute is the object of metaphysical aspiration and God is of religious aspiration.

According to him, there are two worlds: the material world that science studies and the spiritual world that the spiritually inclined perceive. He calls it transcendence or infinite aspect of soul. Upanishads speak of it as "*sarvam khalvidam Brahma*" – everything permeated by Brahman or the spirit which cannot be perceived in any other way. This spirit comes to its fullest expression in human who has a unique position. According to him, human is a peculiar combination of egoism and self-transcendence, of selfishness and universal love. This is due to finite and infinite aspects in human. Thus, human has a special role in creation. Human is a being capable of self-transcendence, self-reflection and planning.

Since human is embodied spirit (finite-infinite, with body and soul), one cannot attain one's ultimate destiny directly. Therefore, the first aspect of one's destiny would be freedom from embodied existence. But, although that may make one free, that will not put an end to creation; and so long as the cosmic process does not come to an end, complete unity will not be established. Therefore, the final aspect of one's destiny must be the realization of unity at the end of the cosmic process. One cannot be free from cosmic process till all others are saved. The world process will reach its final goal when every individual will realize Divinity. Radhakrishnan calls it '*Sarvamukti.*' Once this is realized, the purpose of creation is fulfilled and everything will go back to Brahman.

Epistemology

Radhakrishnan accepts three sources of knowledge - sense experience, intellectual cognition (discursive reasoning) and intuitive apprehension. Sense experience acquaints us with the outer characteristics of the external world. We come to know the sensible qualities of the objects. The data yielded by sense experience constitute the subject matter of natural science. Discursive reason or what Radhakrishnan calls logical knowledge depends on analysis and synthesis of the data of perception. He calls logical knowledge indirect and symbolic. We are able to handle and control the objects of nature with such knowledge. Logical knowledge and sense-experience are the means by which we are capable of practical purposes and control over our environment.

Though he accepts the two means of knowledge, they fail to reveal the "original integrity of the perceived object". Intellectual symbols cannot represent perceived realities, as what they are. Moreover, the entire life of feeling and emotion, 'the delights and pains of the flesh, the agonies and raptures of the soul' remain out off from thought. He thinks of a higher mode of apprehension where thought, feeling and volition are blended into a whole, where there is no duality, the distinction between the knowledge of a thing and its being. It is a type of knowing by becoming. Radhakrishnan calls it Intuitive Apprehension. In the intuitive apprehension, the knower establishes an identity with the known. This can be made clear by taking the example of anger. No intellectual deliberation can give us any idea of the emotion of anger. We can know it only by being angry. Thus, we say intuition establishes a unity – almost an identity between the knower and the known. The object known is seen not as an 'object outside the self, but as a part of the self'. The ultimacy of intuition is also accounted for by Radhakrishnan in that it is the ground of all other forms of experience. Intuition is ineffable. It escapes the limits of language and logic. In such experiences, thought and reality come together. Intuition is the ultimate form of experience for Radhakrishnan. It is ultimate in the sense that intuition constitutes the fullest and therefore the most authentic realization of the Real (Brahman).

Religion and Ethics

Radhakrishnan's ethical teachings must be understood from the background of his religious faith and metaphysics. Every philosophy and religion begins with an intuition. When there is need of explaining intuition to others, need of language comes up. When we speak of Religion, as Radhakrishnan understands it, we must make a distinction between Religion and religions. Religion for him is personal intuitive experience. It is an insight into the nature of reality (*darśana*) and experience of reality (*anubhava*). It is an inward and personal experience which unifies all values and organizes all experiences. It is the reaction to the whole of reality by the whole human. In his book, *Idealistic View of Life,* he calls it spiritual life, the culmination of intellectual, moral and aesthetic activity or a combination of them.

Different religions according to him are different explanations of this experience. In the course of time, in its effort to explain the intuitive experience there came up external structures in the form of rites, ceremonies, institutions, programs etc. When a person experiences within the abounding vitality that transcends consciousness, a new humility is born in the soul. It cleanses the person of pride, prejudice, privilege thoughts and creates a feeling of tenderness and compassion for one's fellow humans. The need of the time is to go from religions to Religion, and for that two things are to be emphasized: inner experience and ethics. Religion also means spirituality which is impossible without ethics, which is the sum total of values and virtues that makes social life smooth and good. He says, 'After all, what counts is not creed but conduct. By their fruits you shall know them and not by their beliefs. Religion is not correct belief but righteous living.'

While speaking about Hindu ethics, Radhakrishnan explains the *puruśārthas* (the four supreme ends of human craving). He writes, 'Ancient Rishis of India' were not only spiritual masters, they were also psychologists, who looked at the motives behind our actions, and they realized that desires or cravings are the very center of our life. Each of these cravings tries for satisfaction. Basically they are four: parental instincts and sexual instincts (*kama*), desire for power and wealth (*artha*), desire for social harmony and common good (*dharma*), and union with the unseen (*mōkṣa*). These desires are not distinct and independent, but always try to win upper hand and win over the other. The greatness of the person consists in making a co-operation of the four and bringing an overarching unity in life. For each one is a whole in oneself.'

Freedom

According to Radhakrishnan freedom is one of the foundations of ethics. Freedom can be understood in three levels. Psychologically it is freedom to act this way or that way. Moral freedom is freedom to choose between alternatives with knowledge and volition. But, here knowledge may not be perfect, so error, evil or ignorance may occur. This is what we see around us. Human made enormous progress in knowledge and scientific inventions. Along with that corresponding moral and spiritual progress has not happened, rather declined in standard. Thus, we must go beyond psychological and moral freedom into spiritual freedom that leads to integral liberation, liberation of the 'whole human', not like economic or political liberation. For the cultivation of a complete human being, we require the cultivation of inward peace, the grace and joy of souls overflowing in love. For this all-round growth needs physical efficiency, intellectual alertness and spiritual awakening.

Radhakrishnan's philosophy can be termed as monistic idealism. He makes a distinction between the Absolute and God. The world is considered as the creative work of God. But, at the same time both God and the world are different. He affirms the spiritual nature of human soul but at the same time gives due respect to the value of the biological aspect of human person. He assumes that the human being is relatively free. He presented his philosophical conviction systematically and with an academic precision.

6.2. Muhammad Iqbal (1876-1938)

Muhammad Iqbal occupies a unique position in the contemporary Indian thought as he tries to apply academic philosophical standards to Islamic thoughts. Iqbal was born in 1876 at Sialkot. He received his early education at Sialkot and Lahore. In 1905, he went to Cambridge. For some time, he did research on Persian metaphysics at Munich in Germany. In 1908, he returned to Lahore and became a barrister. He became very famous as a poet and showed a greater interest in philosophical pursuits. The reconstruction of religious thought in Islam was one of the important aims of his philosophical thinking. Persian philosophy also made a great impact in shaping his philosophy. He was also influenced by Islamic mysticism, especially, by Sufism. Apart from these, his contact with the western philosophical world also molded his philosophy. He died in 1938 at Lahore.

Epistemology

For Iqbal, the ultimate truths are not known by us in the ordinary way, i.e., the way of experience. Experience is conditioned by space-time and is useful only from the empirical and pragmatic point of view. But the reality, in itself, cannot be directly known in this level of experience. As the Quranic idea goes he says that the heart is a kind of inner intuition or insight that takes us to the aspects of Reality. The heart is the faculty of intuition and intuition is the way through which Reality can be apprehended directly. The important character of intuition is its immediacy. Intuition is the immediate knowledge of the Reality. Intuitive knowledge is always a unity or wholeness which is not analyzable. In intuition the knower becomes one with the known. The distinction between the subject and the object disappears altogether. Intuition is a moment of intimate relationship with the Supreme. It is a feeling of the presence of the Divine. According to Iqbal, this intuitive experience has objectivity. It is neither a subjective state nor merely a private and personal experience. As the object of the intuition is not the mere creation of the individual's intellect the object of the experience is really there. He also says that the intuitive experience helps one realize eternity in a moment. He speaks of the incommunicable nature of this intuitive experience. It is not communicable because of the simple reason that it is the function of the heart. He also says that though the content of this experience cannot be communicated, a mystic can interpret this experience and this interpreted truth can be easily communicated.

Concept of God

Iqbal expounded firm conviction on monotheism understandably from his Islamic background. The question of God is important as it satisfies both human religious quest and metaphysical curiosity. There is a Being directing the creative life of the universe and guiding the creative progress of the world. The attributes of God could be apprehended by intuitive insight and through intellectual deliberations. Creativeness, knowledge, omnipotence, eternity, immanence, transcendence etc. are some of the main attributes of God. The attribution of omnipotence to God raises the question of presence of evil in the world. He solves this problem by explaining the concept of freedom given to human by God for making it possible for him/her to bring out the potentialities latent in human beings. At the same time, human can use this freedom rightly or misuse this freedom for wrong choice. He considers that freedom is a basic requirement for goodness. Iqbal considers pain and suffering as the necessary aspects of the fact of freedom. He likes to treat both good and evil within the same whole.

Iqbal treats God's eternity neither as a time concept nor as an idea of endlessness of time. God is considered eternal because He is the expression of the infinite possibilities latent in God. In this sense God is portrayed as eternal. According to Iqbal, God is both immanent and transcendent. But, God is not immanent in the world as a pantheist understands. He is immanent in the world in the sense that the world is His creation. God is presented as transcendent in the sense that the God is beyond the grasp of the finite ego. So, by way of presenting God as a unity of infinite possibilities, the metaphysical demand of human being is satisfied. And by conceiving God as personal and Supreme Ego, the religious demand is also satisfied.

Understanding of Self

Iqbal says that the self is the principle of unity in the individual. He prefers to use the word 'ego' for the self and asserts the necessity to accept the reality of the self. He explains that no mental state can exist in isolation, but there must be a unity organizing all the mental states. This principle of unity of inner life or of the mental state is called as ego. It is the ego which keeps all experiences organized and united. It shows that it is the ego which organizes and gives a final shape and directions to our various affections and experiences.

According to Iqbal, Ego cannot remain in complete isolation, it must have a world. The ego is confronted with the world of non-ego, and it is through his experience of the world of the non-ego that the life of the ego grows and develops. We have seen that all the experience is organized by ego. The ego has the capacity to choose its course of action and thereby ego is free. The self is immortal in spite of its apparent fact of death. The self has the capacity to survive death and thereby, it is immortal. According to Iqbal the realization of immortality is considered as the ultimate human destiny. Immortality is presented both as soul's nature and as a person's destiny. Death is not the end of the soul. The soul survives the death and continues to exist even after death. According to Quran, immortality does not mean attaining godhood. There is no possibility of its return to the earth. It implies that once the soul is free from the body, a person is free from the bondage of birth or re-birth and awaits the final judgment with regard to his\her destiny. So, it does not involve a belief in rebirth.

The Nature of the World

Iqbal asserts the reality of the world. The external world exists and is real. Space and time are relative. They are relative not only to the different grades of being but also to the different levels of experience of the same being. The world is conceived as a continuous movement. He says that even though one finds diverse and discrete aspects of the universe, there exists an inner unity among them all. It has a reason, purpose and a plan and steadily progresses towards the realization of an end.

Iqbal is a mystic philosopher. Intuition alone manifests the truth of God and nature. It gives an organic knowledge. It reveals the nature of ego and helps communion with God. God evolves with the cosmos. He is potentially Infinite and is the conscious force. God is duration and there is no limit for his creativity. The relation between the God and ego is that of a garland with its beads. For him, the external world exists and it is real. The ultimate human destiny is the realization of immortality. Death is not the end and the soul survives death.

6.3. Other Academic Thinkers

K. C. Bhattacharya (1875-1949)

Kalichandra Bhattacharya influenced great number of Indian thinkers in contemporary period. His writings had critical studies of various philosophers and his attempts at personal philosophical synthesis. His method was not mere objective exposition or interpretation, but speculative reconstruction. Philosophy has its place in theoretical consciousness which is the understanding of the speakable. It has a 'believed content' because what is spoken must be in the first instance believed. It is first concerned with understanding of the speakable, not with 'knowing.' In his understanding of the Absolute, first he sees it as the indefinite; then as the subject or 'self, as freedom, then as alternation. The absolute in the final stage as alternation, cannot be known or spoken of except in a purely symbolic manner; language can never explain the Absolute; we can only try to reach it through alternative ways of approaching it. Following the three modes of human consciousness; knowing, feeling and willing, there are three alternative ways of approaching the absolute; the absolute can be seen as truth, freedom and love (value). Knowing leads to the self-evident content, willing leads to consciousness as freedom from content, value or love leads to the unity and indetermination of the content of consciousness. While seeing the absolute as truth-freedom, love, we should not try to see it as a unity of these three as *sat-cit-ānanda* is reconciled in a higher unity in Non-dualism. One has to accept them as irreducible alternatives.

T. M. P. Mahadevan (1911-1983)

Mahadevan was faithful to the original insight of Advaita and tried to show how Advaita gives place to a morality of commitment to the world and yet goes beyond morality. He refused to admit Advaita as definite philosophy: "Advaita does not profess to formulate conceptually what reality is. It is not therefore a system of thought and it only seeks to transcend all views, since these are by their very nature, restricted, limited and circumscribed." Thus, various philosophical views can find their place in it. Advaita is all comprehensive, accommodating varying perspectives and eventually transcending all of them. Vedantic answer provides a deeper solution to the philosophical questions of modern man. Philosophy helps man with inward path in the discovery of meaning of man. He rejects the critics that Indian approach gives no place for morality and social commitment. Spiritual quest of man demands a sound morality yet goes beyond morality; morality is not a realm that is sufficient and self-complete; one has to go beyond ethics to reach the final goal, which is reached only in the plenary experience of spiritual freedom, an experience in which all contradictions are resolved since we have reached pure non-duality.

M. Hiriyanna (1871-1950)

He had been a representative of a value-oriented re-interpretation of advaita. True aim of philosophy is to discover the nature of and devise a suitable means for attaining the highest human values. Philosophy is both a theoretical and a practical task. Theoretical is the determination of the exact nature of the highest values. Practical is to devise suitable means to pursue the highest value. By seeing philosophy as pursuit of value, its role remains as a search for facts; knowledge of facts is not opposed to the search for values. Knowledge is sterile if not linked with practical purposes. Core of his philosophy of value is in the concept of self-perfection. Man, with his capacity of self-criticism points to a standard by which he judges; this standard can be nothing short of absolute perfection. This ideal is however not explicitly known; one can approach this ultimate end by considering the scope and nature of tentative ends likes goodness, beauty and truth. Hiriyanna analyses these three and concludes that they cannot stand for the ultimate end. None of them is ultimate in the sense of an all-sufficing or absolute value. All are ultimate in the sense of being fundamental; each appeals to a distinctive side of man's spiritual nature; all these three are included in the ultimate value yet the ultimate is not a mere combination but represents a creative synthesis of them by which they are fused and welded into a new unity. Hiriyanna finds in self-perfection the ultimate value. This ideal is characterized by absolute unselfishness and spontaneous and permanent joy. It is achieved by a combined pursuit of three values of beauty, truth and goodness. This ideal goal is best expressed in the concept of *mokṣa*.

P. T. Raju (1904-1992)

Raju was trained in western style, influenced by Hegelian philosophy. Later he turned his attention towards humanism. Philosophy is critical-integral humanism or more simply critical humanism. He sought to link philosophy and conduct of life. 'Philosophy has to start from where we stand in this world of finitude but its role is to guide us to a higher level of existence. Finitude is a fact, our chief concern is to know the higher and rise to that life.' Raju tends to place man at the center of philosophy. 'The being of man must be the basis and starting point of philosophy. The ultimate ingredients of his being must be critically understood and their value and validity must be recognized for both theoretical and practical philosophy.

Man searches for truth and for a criterion of truth; Truth is reached not by mere rational coherence, but by transcendental intuition, yet it has to be in some way controlled by reason which plays a critical role in relation with the intuition of truth. Reality is equated with truth, but since truth is beyond thought this identification cannot be an identification of thought and reality as Hegel suggests. Truth or reality can be identified with the Absolute. As Śankara, Raju considers absolute as both indeterminate and indescribable. The basic problem of relationship between the infinite and the finite can find no answer at the level of thought; the concept of *māya* expresses this human incapacity to explain the relationship between finite infinite, rest-change, etc. Finally, reality appears as the ultimate subject, the ultimate self.

Debiprasad Chattopadhyaya (1918-1993)

D. P. Chattopadhyaya was a philosopher outstanding for application of Marxism to the study of Indian philosophy, as seen especially in his book on *Lokayata*. He notes that an interpretation of a given system is always influenced by the standpoint of the interpreter. So, far the history of Indian thought has been mostly done by people belonging to the idealist tradition. His approach can be seen as a corrective and at the same time as an attempt to establish the relevance of the Marxian approach as applied to Indian thought. His approach does not start from any presupposed philosophical conclusion but rather from a methodological presupposition. In the idealist approach a philosophy could be analyzed with very little reference to the social set up in which it had grown. The method which he suggests is to place back philosophy where it belongs, in its socio-economic context. His conclusion is that we can find a form of 'proto materialism in Indian thought' and from this we can conclude that spiritualism is not co extensive with Indian thought and therefore spiritualism is not an eternal adjunct of human history and need not have more than a passing role to play.

Rajendra Prasad (1884-1963)

Rajendra Prasad tried to philosophize mostly in the context of analytical tradition. Among various approaches to language analysis, he uses functional analysis of language. The way to discover the meaning of an expression is to watch its function in its real use. He rejects the theory that all the functions of language can be reduced to one or two functions, however, he suggests that we can broadly classify these functions into two groups; the cognitive and the non-cognitive. A function is cognitive when it is uttered with the primary purpose of conveying information of any kind. Its function is non cognitive in all other uses. Often the same expression can be used to perform various functions, cognitive and non-cognitive. In this case, we can classify it according to its primary purpose in a given situation. He was interested in studying the language of ethics. Following a functional analysis of language he noted that the language of values has to be defined with reference to its purpose or function. Applying this norm to the language of moral values he finds that the general purpose is to persuade others or even oneself; he develops accordingly his persuasion theory of moral language.

Daya Krishna (1924-2007)

Daya Krishna as a professor of philosophy and research fellow in various capacities have offered a counter perspective to all assumed presuppositions of Indian thinkers. Contemporary thinkers have approached and presented Indian philosophy as centered around *moksa,* spiritualism, *astika-nastika* division of Indian systems, theories of *karma* and *purusartha*, etc. Daya questions these assumptions and pose a strong challenge to preconceived and non-critical approach to Indian philosophy. His articulation breaks the traditional frame of doing philosophy in India as just presenting, interpreting or re-interpreting the old ideas. Without rejecting the need for establishing a living continuity with India's philosophical past, his critique of Indian philosophy and thinkers makes it relevant to present times. He tried to relieve traditions from spiritualism. The interest of western Indological studies coupled with the search for a spiritual self-identity in the face of overwhelming western superiority in all fields of knowledge seemed to have led to the creation of certain picture of Indian past. We never tend to question such projection. In his works, Daya has sought not only to break the picture of Indian philosophy but also to relate philosophical past to the active philosophical concerns of contemporary period. Rootedness to the past is needed; but contemporary Indians find their roots not in their own but in the western past traditions. The past intellectual traditions are not sought out of mere historical curiosity. Relating to the past is for re-establishing a living continuity with it to make it relevant today.

Chapter 7

RELIGIOUS AND SPIRITUAL MASTERS (GURUS)

Throughout the history of India, emerged gurus and god-men who interpreted human existence. The Gurus and several god-men and women of today have a variety of interpretation of human existence and adopt a syncretistic way to tackle the problems of everyday life. Religious teachers have been numerous in contemporary India and abroad. Many of them offer no deep system of thought. Yet we underline here some of the significant contributions of contemporary masters. Most of them find their place in the context of Advaitic tradition. They could be divided into two groups: those following the strict, orthodox advaitic teachings and those who reinterpret the tradition. The most orthodox form of advaitic teaching is found in Ramana Maharishi, Sai Baba, Sivananda and Chinmayananda. Bhaktivedanta and the Hare Krishna movement take a complete distance from the advaitic tradition; they see advaita as an error and a form of atheism; they find their place in the great teacher of the tradition of Caitanya. Similarly, Osho cannot be considered as part of the advaitic tradition although one might hesitate to put him in any given tradition; he finds some inspiration from the tantric tradition but his synthesis seems to elude any formal categorization. J. Krishnamurti is even more radical in rejecting all traditions and in trying to find a tradition-free teaching. His quest for truth tries to free itself from every reference to other traditions.

7.1. Ramana Maharshi (1879-1950)

Venkataraman was born on 30th December 1879 at Tiruccuzhi near Madurai in Tamil Nadu, to Sundaram and Azhagammal. There was nothing markedly distinctive about Venkataraman's early years. During his school days, he was an indifferent student, not at all serious about his studies. It was apparently by accident that he heard about Arunacala mountain when he was sixteen years of age. He read *Periyapuranam,* which contains lives of the Saiva saints. The example of the saints fascinated him and he longed to have spiritual experience. He set out for Arunacala and reached Tirumanamalai, in North Tamil Nadu. Involving himself in deep meditation, he attracted many local and foreign disciples. He lived in an ashram and taught his disciples.

Ramana seldom wrote and what little he did write in prose or verse was written to meet the specific demands of his devotees. The most important of his works, is *The Forty Verses on Existence.* His *Upadesasaram* sets forth the quintessence of Vedānta. He rendered into Tamil, two works of Śaṅkarā, like *Vivekacudamani* and *Atmabodha.*

Advaitic Teaching

Ramana's teaching is basically a statement of Advaita philosophy, using the good illustration of cinema for the illusory character of the world. We think that what happens on the screen is real but in fact only the screen is real and the image cannot exist independently of the screen. The Self: the search for the reality of the self leads to differentiate the self from whatever is finite and identify it with the infinite. The basic question a disciple has to ask himself is 'who am I?'. To answer this question, the self eliminates all that is unnecessary and comes to see himself as pure awareness. The self cannot remain at this pure level; soon thought arises and the first thought is the thought of 'I'. Man usually continues in a process of externalization and comes to see a whole world. The process that leads to spiritual realization is a process of inwardness. In this process of inwardness, I come to this fundamental intuition that the self is identical with the absolutes. The self is that where there is absolutely no 'I' thought. That is called silence. The self itself is the world, the self itself is 'I' the self itself is God, all is Siva, the self. So, the ultimate truth of the self is that it is 'essential being'.

Self-Realization

His philosophy provides a background for the practical task of self-realization. As we have seen this self-realization comes by destroying the mind. This can be realized directly through *jñāna* or indirectly through yoga and the control of the breath. Of these two, Ramana prefers the more direct method of *jñāna.* The method of *jñāna* is achieved through self-inquiry. By it man is liberated simply by becoming aware that there was no bondage. For undertaking this inquiry, one must possess a sharp mind – much sharper than the one required for unravelling the mysteries of Matter. It is with the one-pointed intellect that the truth is to be seen. It is true that even the intellect will have to get resolved before the final wisdom dawns. But, up to that point it has to inquire and inquire relentlessly. Wisdom, surely, is not for the indolent. The cessation or non-cessation of the body has nothing to do with release. They may continue to exist and the world may continue to appear. That makes no difference at all to the Self that has been realized. In truth, there is neither the body nor the world for him. We have that experience in sleep where we are conscious neither of the external world of things nor of the inner world of dreams.

Critically viewing, his philosophy would not easily lead to a practical commitment to the world. Ramana's world-denying philosophy leads to a constant denial that there is any objective problem to be solved. When disciples ask him what attitude we should have towards human suffering he simply argues that one is not aware of the suffering of the world when he sleeps. 'When you remain as the self, as in sleep, the world and its suffering will not affect you.' Similarly, to people who try to change society he says, 'why do you exert yourself so much to effect reform? Go to sleep and see if there are differences. There you obliterate differences without any effort.' Pushing to its logical conclusion his own position he says, 'the loss of one or several or all lives either in this world or in all three worlds makes no difference.'

7.2. Jiddhu Krishnamurthi (1895-1986)

Jiddu Krishnamurti was born on May 11, 1895 in Chennai. Ms. Annie Besant took him as her adopted child and sent him to England for studies. In 1911, he was proclaimed head of the newly established order of the star of the East and as a 'World Teacher.' In England rich ladies took care of his education in tutorial institutions. As he did all his studies privately, he made a fierce attack on formal learning. At 16, Krishnamurti delivered his first lecture at Varanasi. Krishnamurti wrote his first book when he was just 15, and it was later published in 27 languages with 40 editions in all. On December 28, 1925, the voice of the 'World Teacher' was heard for the first time at Adyar. Happiness was his message. Experience was his watchword and suffering was his cry. In 1929, at the age of 34, Krishnamurti renounced all claims to divinity and bade farewell to theosophical society. Throughout his life, he lectured mostly abroad, and he died in U.S.A., on February 17, 1986. The fascinating personality of Krishnamurti attracted many intellectuals from the East and the West. He had many listeners and admirers in Europe and America but very few in India were attracted to him. Here was a Hindu rebel preaching Spiritual anarchy. Indian intelligentsia considered him as a Westerner with Indian Skin.

'Guru Within You'

Jiddu Krishnamurti cannot be called a 'philosopher' in the technical, western sense of the term; he has no systematic or organized thought pattern. He deliberately refused to follow any of the systematical thought of the East or of the West. His uniqueness consists in his ruthless rejection of systematic thought or its expression. He followed nobody as his guru and he did not want to be called a guru. "The guru is within you," he used to say often. He has no teaching to give. For him, truth is self-awareness and self-knowledge. His mission is only to awaken the mind of people to a genuine search for truth and to cure them from the false ways in which they have been made to search. No one can borrow the teaching of another. Everyone has to be his own master. Krishnamurti drew all his inspiration from the book of nature. He would never quote any text, sacred or secular. All his thoughts flowed from inner, personal reflection and insights, intuitions. For Krishnamurti, nature reflected the truth of life. Says Krishnamurti: "I am not a Hindu or anything else, for I do not belong to any group, religious or otherwise."

Concept of God

Krishnamurti traces belief in God to man's sense of despair to get rid of despair, man puts his trust and hope in a personal God who will protect him in troubled times. Says Krishnamurti: "God is the illusion we worship and the non-believer creates the illusion of another god which he worships the State or some other utopia or some book which he think contains all truth". To be really religious, we must free ourselves from this concept of God and its illusion. As regards the origin of belief in God, Krishnamurti says that it arises from fear and uncertainty about our future and our sense of insecurity. Krishnamurti says that when a man is unable to cope with fear, it engenders dependence on a supernatural power and this sense of fear and dependence creates in our mind the idea of God. Says Krishnamurti: "Belief in God comes from fear and it is the most destructive thing. One must free oneself from fear and from belief. Religious belief divides people, makes them hard, makes them hate each other and cultivate war." In fear and religious belief, the human mind is unable to understand truth.

Religion and Human Freedom

Man's quest is for freedom and freedom comes through understanding. Authority denies this process. He warns man against the danger of religions and religious teachers. Religions appears as an expression to the neurotic state of man. Man wants to live in unity and harmony. He finds that reality is fragmented. Man wants to escape this fragmentation. He invents myths and religions to help him escape, but by this same act he escapes from reality. Krishnamurti vehemently condemned a world-negating, otherworldly spirituality; He called it distortion of religion. He said: "We cannot live without matter and life is not possible without persons and things. What is important is the totality of life" when we divide the religious life from the worldly, we create conflict. A life of conflict is not religious life. He declared: "I want to free man from the chains of fear. I am not to found a new religion. My only purpose is to free man completely.

Religion is to be as search for reality. The discovery leads to true goodness and love. Religion is not the art of cultivation of virtues; it is enough to be aware of the real. It is the feeling of being completely good not the cultivation of goodness. The ideal of religion is not moral. 'not what man ought to be but rather a realization of what he is. He came down heavily on the traditional Guru-Sisya concept, since, for him, this method obstructed true learning, which presupposes full freedom on the part of the students. Krishnamurti rejected all forms of organized religions, since, according to him, they obstructed the free flow and expression of truth, which is nothing but consciousness of the totality of existence, while organized religions are opposed to it.

Humans and their World

Regarding the quality of human life, Krishnamurti had very clear but radical ideas. He says that we must live without any fixed pattern, without goal, without hope, above all, without any conflict. We must live the present meaningfully and fully. There should not be any life transcendence or suppression of life. According to him, fear is the greatest problem in the world, probably, the greatest problem. One destroys oneself by thinking of the future, he advised his listeners to live in the present. New human beings are those who are fully freed from the weight of time past, says Krishnamurti. Regarding conflict he says that during the 5000 years of recorded history, human have fought about 5000 wars, and this is still going on. It shows that human society is neurotic. Because of human divisive tendencies, he says that the whole world is broken up outwardly, as men are broken up inwardly. "This outer fragmentation is the manifestation of the human being's inner division."

Choiceless Awareness

The fundamental change needed in the psychic structure of human being, Krishnamurti terms as 'mutation of mind,' 'psychological revolution,' and 'transformation of consciousness.' To him, there is only consciousness; the divisions in consciousness in terms of the self and the nonself, you and me, individual and collective, conscious and unconscious and so on, are classifications of thought for the convenience of understanding and for the sake of communicating such understanding. All divisions are arbitrary and conventional. He perceives life essentially focused in the individual. If one is clear within oneself, one can begin to show a different way of life free from fear, from duality and form identification with idea. For him, to be is to be related. Existence by itself implies relationship. One cannot think of exclusively individual existence in terms of consciousness. In our day to day life, existence is reduced to be the struggle for survival. The problem is by making the individual as the absolute which leads to self-identification and the establishment of consciousness exclusive, although existence is essentially relative. Such fragmentation of consciousness becomes the fundamental problem of human existence.

To set right the problem Krishnamurti offers a solution through the understanding or awareness of the real. The real cannot be described in words but the real comes into being. When one becomes aware of 'what is' of the actual, that is when one is free from the ideal, from 'what should be' one understands the real. 'What is' is to be seen in the mirror of relationship. It cannot be understood in withdrawal, in isolation. "The 'what is' can be understood only when the mind is utterly passive, when it is not operating on what is." (*Commentaries on Living,* 63) Understanding is passive awareness, direct perception, without implying time and effort, without the interference of thought. Choiceless awareness is the crucible which dissolves every problem effortlessly. Krishnamurti focusses his attention on the silence of mind as the solution of the problem of existence. By the silence of mind what he means is the cessation of choice, the freeing of attention from concentration on the opposites, freedom from fear and from self-perpetuative thought. The mind is always busy, chattering, wanting, identifying, occupied with becoming this or that. This preoccupation of the mind with the ideal, with what should be is a hindrance to the perception of truth. Thought cannot solve our problems. Cessation of thought brings about the silence of mind. In that silence there is a direct and simple perception of the whole problem. "Thought can only come to an end when the thinker understands himself. The thinker and the thought are not two separate processes. The thinker is the thought." (*Talks,* Madras, 1947, 103) Choice is conditional thinking. Therefore, according to Krishnamurti, truth can only be discovered in the 'choiceless awareness' of the psychological structure of the self, of the limitation of the conditioned existence.

Jiddu Krishnamurti is a free thinker of international reputation. His thinking is free from the conditioning influences of the different systems of philosophy, religious dogmatism, political ideology, intellectual speculation and cultural bias. He opens a new chapter in the history of Indian philosophy and religion. He earnest wishes to have enquiry into the nature of existence and reality without any presumption or assumptions. His approach to understand life is direct and simple. He presupposes no other training needed than a pure heart and simple mind. His teaching is like a finger pointing to the experience of Wisdom dawning upon human consciousness.

7.3. Osho Rajneesh (1931-1990)

Rajneesh Chandra Mohan Jain was born in Kuchiwada, Madhya Pradesh on 11 December, 1931 in an ordinary middle class. During his boyhood he showed a deep and penetrating understanding of spiritual matters and developed a critical attitude towards dogmatic beliefs, blind faith and meaningless rituals. He did his M.A. in Philosophy from Sagar University. He was professor of philosophy in Rani Durgawati University at Jabalpur. He took touring different places delivering discourses. He grew to be a spiritual revolutionary. He tried to pulverize dogma bound religious pundits and dismantled the edifices of religious beliefs. Having found that professorship was secondary in his life work, he resigned the job and started initiating his followers into '*sanyās*,' in Bombay. He started vigorous mediation camps showering love and benediction. In 1974, he established a small Commune in Koregaon Park, Poona that attracted many foreigners. The ashram offered yoga classes and allied therapies and offered a permissive atmosphere. He was called first Acharya Rajneesh then Bhagwan Shree Rajneesh (till 1988) and from 1989 till his death, Osho. In his discourse erudite scholarship, power of expression, making the abstruse seemingly simple and easy, talks with humour and rare wit, speaking from the heart, kade him immensely love, adored and venerated. He claimed to be the guru, the spiritual teacher of modern India. His journey of life ended on 19 January, 1990.

Critique of Religions

Osho has been a source of inspiration. During his discourses of the subjects, he touched were countless. Criticizing some religions which are based on fear; fear of the supernatural; of the other world; of unknown forces of nature; of non-terrestrial beings, Osho views that religions are based on human psychological need of security. The child needs security and parents provide it. Osho calls such religions as the teddy bear type of religion. The child finds comfort and security in the toy in absence of parents. Religions have treated humans children, threatening with fears of many things as well as providing them comfort and security. Many men/women grow depending on 'teddy bear' like Gods. He calls this type of religion as neurotic religion, a negation of religion. True religion is joy-filled positive affirmation of humans.

Life as Celebration

Rajneesh wanted to create a "new man" combining the spirituality of Buddha, of Krishna, of Christ, of Zarathustra, of Tao, of Zen, of Tantra and of Upaniṣads. The zest for life is exemplified by traditions with a full integration of matter and spirit. His approach was syncretistic and highlighted meditation, awareness, love creativity and humor which found unquestioned acceptance among his followers. Osho said, "I teach you life, I teach you love, I teach you how to sing, how to dance. I teach you how to transform your life into a festival, into a carnival of delight, hence laughter has to be one of the most essential qualities." For him, life as celebration leads us to God.

Among his many original spiritual thoughts, one is Osho's urge and ability to just laugh, with reason or even when there is no reason at all. When a religion is alive laughter is the prayer. When it is dead religion becomes an enemy of laughter. Laughter is the throb of life. A religion can transform the world with language of laughter, of song, of dance, merry making and celebration. If the smile, the laughing, the joyful attitude is integrated in our lives the state of '*samadhi* ' and,'*moksa*' is achieved. One who knows how to laugh, even his tears are joyful. If laughter is to just forget one's woes, distress, misery then it is only an opiate, without any spiritual value. To Osho, the humour, laughter is a source of positive joy, happiness and bliss. It is a medium by which one's inner ecstacy is given outer manifestation. It is divine.

Simple joyful expression of love is everybody's way to happiness. Life is full of little tid -bits, full of opportunity to provoke merriment but we are unconcernexd and pay not the least heed. Life is a celebration of thoughts, feelings, creative sentiments, marvellous pleasant dreams, happiness, enthusiasm and awareness. The greatest search of all living forms has been the seeking of happy life – a life full of joy, of plenty, of no mental anxiety or stress. The entire Existence is saturated with bliss, ecstacy, '*anand*' but we never stop and drink the nectar. Osho says, every experience, every despair, every disappointment can be so lived that life continues as a celebration, a festivity, a rejoicing. The unhappiness has no relation to reality. We have to be silently drinking the beauty of existence all around. Possession is useless greed, sharing is blissful.

Osho was a "freethinking agnostic" and enjoys wide recognition as thinker, writer and orator. Critics diverge in their appraisal as some hail him as the 20th century's greatest spiritual teacher as well as the one of the most maligned figures in history. His ideas on sex, family and human relationships roused opposition and severe critics in India and abroad.

7.4. Sathya Sai Baba (1926-2011)

Sai Baba was a well revered guru and religious leader. He was born on 23 November, 1926 in Puttaparthi in Andhra, as a fourth child to Vekkappa Raju and Eswaramma. He was named as Sathya Narayan Raju. His father was a farmer of a very ordinary lower middle class family. The family had rich musical, literary and dramatic traditions. At the age of fourteen, he claimed that he was in fact the incarnation of Sai Baba of Shirdi who prophesied before his death in 1918 that he would be born again. In 1968, during a discourse in Goa he disclosed that he belonged to the clan of Bhardwaj Rishi securing the great boon from Siva. In 1940, he felt himself detached from family bonds and started living outside the village. He started teaching people sacred *bhajans* and devoted thronged to him. In 1949, a separate ashram was built and named as *praśānti nilayam* – abode of peace. He declared his mission, "to reconstruct the ancient highway to God; to fulfil a task of spiritual regeneration of humanity through truth and love; to foster the Vedas and devotees; to achieve the supreme task of uniting as one family the entire mankind, through the bond of brotherhood."

He was hailed as a god-man and miracle worker. He was believed by many of possessing the miraculous characteristics, powers and glory of an *avatar* of God. He advocated values of truth, right conduct, non-violence, love and peace – *satya, dharma, ahimsa, prema and śānti.* To spread his ideals, he established more than thousand Sai Samitis (centers) across the world, with millions of adherents who consider him as an *avatar* of Sai Baba of Shirdi. Besides speaking on spiritual values, his fame comes from his social activities, especially in rural development, education and health care. He established education institutes, emphasizing the pursuit of academic excellence. His system of integral education is designed to foster self-discipline and pro-social conduct. For him, end of education is character formation. All his social activities aimed at providing all basic requirements for maintenance of human life.

Service to Humanity

Baba lays great emphasis on social service to humanity. He teaches that His mission is to help humans to understand better themselves as possessing, each of them, a spark of the divine. He teaches to work together and serve each other so that mankind can live, finally, in a world community governed by love, cooperation, and concern for each other's well-being. At the man's center is his divine self. World community is what is needed. Modern conditions suggest the requirement of a world outlook, a world view. A world community is called for and eventually must be built. Human love must be expressed and made the heart of human relations in all societies and the world. We are all interconnected. Changes proposed to make world community to emerge are firstly to share human love towards one another; secondly towards human sharing and human service; thirdly towards discipline; fourthly toward responsibility to one's self, to one's integral community and to the world of humans as a whole.

Towards Universal Religion

To define universal religion is to confine it to a set of theological doctrines. Universal religion defies all definitions and outgrows the narrow confines of the doctrines of any single living religion. It must be universal in intent and outlook. It is happily free from any doctrinal rigidity and is good to all, intended for all and is available to all. It is a quintessence of the spirit of all living religions, without their fanaticism and frantic eagerness to convert others. The supreme message is message of love based on faith in the 'fatherhood of God and brotherhood of man.' For Sai Baba, three most prominent avenues to realization of the ideal of establishing the universal religion are; 1) to get the whole of humankind to rally round one spiritual genius and owe its absolute allegiance to him; 2) to pursue unifying movements based on the syncretistic elements available in all religions; 3) to pursue a comparative study of all living religions and discover the fundamental and unifying core of all faiths hidden deep under the superficial patterns of diversity of rituals, traditions and doctrines. In the person of Sai Baba we find a spiritual genius who can rally round Him men of different faiths. He has told his followers never to give up their faith in their traditional Gods. His mission is to subordinate the superficial layers of differences and to unify all creeds into one supreme religion, the religion of love and brotherhood. In fact every religion has its inherent and in-built factors conducive to a sense of unity. Besides synthesizing tendencies displayed by individual religions there have been collective efforts to ensure a sense of oneness of humanity and to establish a kind of universal religion. By underlining the common core of all religions in his discourses, Sai Baba insisted on forgetting the differences and live in peace.

Chapter 8

INDIAN CHRISTIAN THINKERS

India as a land of religions, provides a background for philosophizing. Doing philosophy in this context has a distinctive flavor. Indian pluralistic set-up in terms of religions, languages, philosophies, political ideologies and ethnicity, influenced Indian Christians considerably. The characteristic mark of Indian Christian thinkers is their concern to make their faith intelligible to the people in India. It took different forms, inculturation, interfaith dialogue and liberalization of the discriminated women, children, poor and dalits.

The process of inculturation is to think and articulate their inherited tradition in Indian symbols and within a philosophical and religious framework. The process led Indian Christians to a deep study of Indian culture and religions. Francis Acharya, Amalorpavadass, Vandana Mataji, Bede Griffifs, Abhishiktananda pioneered this effort. In this process of philosophizing they entered into dialogue with non-Christian community. The thinkers focused on interfaith dialogue, bringing about a wide spectrum of views among them. The major discovery in this development was that it made them self-critical of their theological positions and absolute claims to truth.

The Indian Christian thinkers also understood their faith commitment in relation to their social reality Christian faith implies justice and concern for the poor. Several thinkers devoted themselves in understanding Kingdom of God in terms of justice. People are freed from all sort of bondage, not merely spiritual, but also material, social, political, economic and cultural. Thinkers like Sathianathan Clarke, Arvind P. Nirmal, Sebastian Kappen, Felix Wilfred addressed several issues like caste system, gender justice, ecology besides the strictly spiritual concerns such as prayer, meditation, liturgy etc. In addressing these concerns they philosophized. Philosophy is making sense of reality with whatever means available, reality that we humans are, the reality that surrounds us and the reality that transcends both these dimensions.

From Indian Christian perspective there are attempts of doing philosophy in different ways. Many tried to synthesize Christian doctrines with Indian Philosophy and Culture, Trinity for instance. Specifically, they took up Christian doctrines and made to interact with Indian philosophy and culture, such that Christianity is presented in an inculturated Indian 'garb.' Others had their focus on certain themes in Indian philosophy and looked for their parallels in Christianity. Interaction between Christian and Indian themes was done, illuminating each with the help of the other and bringing about a new synthesis. This exercise needs a very high level of philosophical competence and scholarship and demands thorough knowledge of both traditions as well as a genius for integration. Thinkers like Raimon Panikkar, Brahmabandhav Upadhyaya, Richard DeSmet, and most recently Francis Xavier D'Sa and John Vattanky contributed much to the shaping of contemporary Christian contribution to Indian Philosophy.

8.1. Raimon Panikkar (1918-2005)

Born on 3 November 1918 in Barcelona to the parents who came from diverse backgrounds, Raimon Panikkar became a reputed figure in the field of theology, philosophy and social thinking. His father was an Indian Hindu and his mother was a Catalan Catholic. Panikkar was ordained a Catholic priest in 1946. Later, he undertook studies in Indian philosophy and religion. For the next fifty years Panikkar pursued his academic career as a professor in European, Indian and North American universities. Some of his works include; *The Unknown Christ of Hinduism, The Trinity and Religious Experience, Worship and Secular Man, The Vedic Experience, Myth, Faith and Hermeneutics, The Intra-religious Dialogue* and *The Cosmotheandric Experience.*

Philosophy and Culture

Raimon Panikkar's primary concern was that of culture, religion and the relationship between the two. For him, religion, philosophy and culture are three "elements" of the human reality. If the first could be compared to the feet with which Man journeys towards his destiny, philosophy could represent the eyes that scrutinize that journey, and culture, the earth on which human being is walking during his/her concrete pilgrimage. One cannot separate Philosophy from Religion, and both are dependent on the culture which nurtures them. Philosophy is the activity by which human being participates consciously and critically, in the discovery of reality. Each culture offers to philosophy the language that is essential for the philosophy to formulate its insights. But, it is the philosophy that tries to question the very foundations on which each culture is based. Philosophy is authentic, revolutionary, protesting and transforming.

In other words, each philosophy emerges from the womb of a culture, and simultaneously by questioning what holds that culture together, can transform it. In fact, every deep cultural change has emerged from philosophical activity. It is philosophers who influence most of the destinies of history.

Interculturality

In today's world, monoculturalism is lethal and multiculturalism is impossible. Interculturality is the philosophical imperative of our times. Interculturality recognizes both assertions and seeks a middle way. Interculturality is inherent to the human being and a unique culture is as incomprehensible and impossible as a single universal language and as one man alone. Interculturality is a possibility situated between two (or more) cultures. We cannot claim to define through one single word what intercultural philosophy is, nor even presuppose that such a philosophy exists. Each culture is a galaxy which secretes its self-understanding, and with it, the criteria of truth, goodness, and beauty of all human actions. There are no cultural universals but surely human invariants. The way human invariant is lived and experienced in each culture is distinct and distinctive in each case. Cultural respect requires that we respect those ways of life that we disapprove, or even those that we consider as pernicious.

Religion

Religion is the path that leads one to the state of fulfillment or salvation. Salvation, understood here in its broadest sense, is anything making one whole, healthy, free, and complete. It could also be understood by different people as heaven, *nirvana*, nothingness, just society, etc. Thus, a religion is that set of practice and/or doctrines which one believes will lead one to the liberation or fulfillment of one's being. These practices and doctrines are spatially, temporally and culturally conditioned. Within each religion one can distinguish three aspects: (1) the socio-historical expressions in and through which a religion is alive, (2) the sacramental or sacred structures that mediate a relationship to the transcendent and (3) the transcendent divine reality, the mystery, the goal of all religions. At the socio-historical level religions are equivalent to each other; at the sacramental level they complement and supplement each other; and the level of the mystery, which is neither one nor many, and which is called by many names and is experienced in many ways, religions bear witness to the infinite richness of the mystery and the impossibility of any one religion to exhaust it. For Panikkar, religions are like the different colors of a rainbow, there are several colors and no color has a monopoly over the others.

Multi-Faith and Dialogical Dialogue

For Panikkar, multi-faith dialogue is highly urgent activity directed towards creating new forms of human consciousness and corresponding new forms of religiousness. It involves the crossing-over of traditions in a manner that does not abandon one's primal tradition, but deepens and extends it. Something new is created at the level of human and religious consciousness. Panikkar's primary principle for religious encounter is that it must be a truly religious experience. According to him, it is more an exchange of religious experiences than of doctrines. The dialogue route is existential, intimate and concrete. Its purpose is not to establish some universal religion. Genuine dialogue between religions, therefore, ought to be this dialogue: between you and me, between you and your neighbour; it should be like a rainbow where we are never sure where one color begins and another ends. It must be free from particular and general apologetics. Those involved in interfaith dialogue should not see their task in terms of defending religion in general against the non-religious or anti-religious attitudes of secular society. Religious encounter is a meeting of persons, not simply the meeting of minds. It is not only a theological symposium but a religious encounter in faith, hope and love.

Dialogical dialogue begins with the assumption that the other is also an original source of human understanding and that, at some level, persons who enter the dialogue have a capacity to communicate their unique experiences and understandings to each other. There are certain indispensable prerequisites for dialogical dialogue. These include a deep human honesty, intellectual openness and a willingness to forego prejudice in the search for truth while maintaining 'profound loyalty towards one's own tradition.' Second, one needs a deep commitment and desire to understand another tradition. Both partners are encouraged to "cross-over" to the other tradition and then "cross back again" to their own. One learns to think and understand on the basis of the symbol systems of more than one tradition. Symbols are both bounded and open. Their interpretation is never exhausted. And yet they are concrete, always tied to a particular worldview.

Concept of Truth

Truth does not allow itself to be conceptualized. It is never purely objective, absolute. To talk about absolute truth is really a contradiction in terms. The pretension of the great religions to possess all truth can only be understood in a limited and contingent context. Not to be conscious of our myths leads to integralism. But in order to be aware of our myths, we need our neighbour, and therefore dialogue and love. The truth is first of all a reality that permits us to live, an existential truth that makes us free. He says that he is not such a relativist as to believe that the truth is cut up in slices like a cake. But, he expresses his conviction that everyone participates in the truth. And the value of dialogue between the various religions is precisely to help me perceive that there are other windows, other perspectives. Therefore, I need the other in order to know and verify my own perspective of the truth. Truth is a genuine and authentic participation in the dynamism of reality. He makes it clear that the dialogue between religions is not a strategy for making one truth triumphant, but a process of looking for it and deepening it along with others.

Humans in Web of Relations

The human being is a person, not an individual. The individual, who is separate from the others, or from the earth or the divine, does not exist. We belong both to earth and to the divine by our very nature. We are conscious and free parts of a whole, but not as puppets that can be easily directed by threads, but rather we find ourselves within a cosmic interweaving or network. "I understand a person as 'a knot in a net' of relationships." These threads connect us with our fellow persons, the earth and divinity. The more conscious the person is, the more he/she realizes that his/her person reaches out to the confines of the world. That is the enlightened man/woman.

Cosmotheandric Vision

Panikkar develops his cosmotheandric vision of reality with reference to three major religious traditions: The Christian Trinity; the Vedanta Hindu *Advaita*; the Buddhist *pratityasamutpada.* He believes that the threefold pattern-traditionally *Theos-anthropos-cosmos*-are invariants of all religions and cultures. He describes the cosmotheandric principle as an intuition of the threefold structure of all reality, the triadic oneness existing on all levels of consciousness and reality. In Christian terms, ultimate reality, the Trinity, is one but also three; in Hindu terms the ultimate unity of all things is literally neither one *(advait)* nor two (*advitya*); in Buddhist terms everything is radically related to everything else (*pratityasamutpada*).

The cosmotheandric principle could be stated by saying that the divine, the human and the earthly are the three irreducible dimensions which constitute the real. Everything that exists, any real being, presents this triune constitution expressed in three dimensions. Panikkar's formulation of reality as *cosmotheandric* challenges the assumption that reality is reducible to Being. there is also Non-Being, the abyss, silence and mystery. We cannot identify even the consciousness with reality because there is also matter and spirit. Panikkar conceives that reality is not mind alone, or *cit*, or consciousness, or spirit. Reality is also *sat* and *ānanda*, also matter and freedom, joy and being. In fact, this is for Panikkar the fundamental religious experience; Being or reality transcends thinking. Panikkar's cosmotheandric vision reveals three assumptions regarding the reality. Firstly, reality is ultimately harmonious.

Secondly, reality is radically relational and interdependent in such a way that every reality is constitutively connected to all other realities. Thirdly, reality is symbolic. We do not have a God separate from the world, a world that is purely material, nor humans that are reducible to their own thought-processes or cultural expressions.

Concept of Theos

The divine dimension of reality is not an 'object' of human knowledge, but the depth-dimension to everything that is. Panikkar does not want to confine the divine mystery into mere God-talk. He identifies divine mystery using non-theistic terms as infinitude, freedom and nothingness. The mystery of the divine is the mystery of the inherent inexhaustibility of all things, at once infinitely transcendent, utterly immanent, totally irreducible, and absolutely ineffable.

Concept of Anthropos

Consciousness is the human dimension of reality which is not reducible to humanity: Consciousness permeates every being. Everything that is, is *consciousness*. In other words, consciousness relates not only to humans who know but to everything else that is actually or potentially known. From the other perspective, if consciousness relates to everything, the human person can be never reduced to consciousness. Panikkar presents human experience as a threefold reality: aesthetic, intellectual and mystical. He critiques technocratic culture for reducing human life to two levels, namely, the sensible and the rational, forgetting the mystical aspect. Panikkar's intention is to show that genuine human experience involves the harmony of senses, intellect and mystical awareness in correlation with matter, thought and freedom. Thought and mystical awareness are not possible without matter, indeed, without the body. All our thoughts, words, states of consciousness and the like are also material, or have a material basis.

He places human person in the context of culture as his main concern was that of interculturalism. For him Man\Woman is a cultural animal. He also believes that culture is not extrinsic to him\her, but natural. He further explains that human is a being that is naturally cultural – or culturally natural. Culture is the field that makes it possible for us to cultivate the world that it itself presents to us, so that man/woman may become fully human and achieve his fullness. Culture is the specific form of human nature. The nature of man/woman is cultural. Culture is neither artificial nor additive to man/woman. The ultimate criterion for condemning another culture will therefore consist in showing that it is anti-natural.

Concept of Cosmos

The world of matter, energy, space and time is our home. These realities are ultimate and irreducible. There is no thought, prayer or action that is not radically cosmic in its foundations, expressions and effects. The earth is sacred. There is something more than pure materiality in a simple stone. Through its existence in space and time, the stone is connected to the entire universe with which it shares its destiny. In Panikkar's terms, there are no disembodied souls or disincarnated gods, just as there is no matter, no energy, no spatio-temporal world without divine and conscious dimensions. Every concrete reality is cosmotheandric - a symbol of the `whole'. It is not only God who reveals; the earth has its own revelations. Matter, space, time and energy are then co-extensive with both human consciousness and the divine mystery.

8.2. Brahmabandhab Upadhyay (1861-1907)

Born a Brahmin, exposed to Christianity, Brahmabandhab Upadhyay did not renounce the cultural and social practices of his caste even while actively involved in Christian leadership. He was influenced by K.C. Sen through Brahma Samaj. He was an enigmatic thinker, trying to reconcile the differences in religions, especially to reconcile the Christian Faith with Hindu philosophical thought. He continuously struggled to enable the point of convergence between Christianity and Hinduism. He was a religious reformer and religious revivalist, a self-confessed 'Hindu-Catholic,' political activist and social commentator. He tried to incorporate the natural theology of Thomas Aquinas in the Vedanta Philosophy. He opined that the catholic faith can be made intelligible to the learned Hindu by adopting the Vedantic philosophy. Thomistic adoption of Aristolelean philosophy remained alien to Hindu minds. Vedanta would serve the purpose. Truths found in Hindu scriptures were developed through the use of reason. It has divine origin. He superimposed revelatory truths of Indian scripture onto Thomistic natural theology, calling it 'rationalist theism.' Vedantic philosophical system should be won over in the service of Christianity as Greek philosophy was in the medieval Christian thought.

He emphasized the Christian faith must fulfill and not destroy what is true and good in Hinduism. As in ancient Greek thought, in Hindu thought, human philosophy or insight into the invisible things of God reached its zenith. The doctrines of Christ, the Trinity, the atonement and the resurrection are supernatural truths beyond the domain of reason. He repudiated the advaitic philosophy and decried the concepts of *maya, rebirth, karma* and attacked polytheism.

His main aim was to construct a Hindu platform of belief and practice to make Christian message intelligible in India. His famous Sanskrit hymn, *vande saccidanandam* is a remarkable allusion to the Holy Trinity, and a pioneering attempt to combine catholic theology with Sanskritic vocabulary. In 1900, he started a new magazine *Sophia* where he wrote on caste seeking a return to what he considered the true, original and still valid insights of the caste system. In 1904, he assumed editorship of *Sandhya*, addressing nationalistic concerns without much of theological and philosophical concerns.

Contribution of Upadhyaya is seen today with the growing openness within Indian Christianity to adopt Indian categories and make the Catholic faith intelligible to non-Catholics. He was a trend-setter in modern quest for interreligious dialogue and inculturality. He remains a living challenge to the alienating modes of Christian behaviour, practice and teaching that had taken root in the land.

8.3. Richard De Smet SJ (1916-1997)

He was a well-known scholar with a systematic and philosophical approach to Hindu-Christian dialogue. Taking up seriously as a young scholastic, study of significance of Vedantic thought, Hindu doctrine and spirituality to Christian theology, he continued his research to the end. De Smet approached Sankara both as an Indologist and a catholic theologian, reconciling the authentic teachings of Sankara with Christian thinking especially of Aquinas, on ontology and liberation.

Thomistic and Advaitic Methods

The similarities in the theological method and doctrine of Sankara and Aquinas, are shown by De Smet. Both subordinate reason to the authority of revealed scripture, make liberation as the ultimate goal of their teaching, liberation as the blissful intellectual experience of the Godhead and the complete cessation of man's ignorance. On the nature of the supreme reality both demonstrate a remarkable convergence. It is characterized as absolutely simple and undivided plentitude of being, transcendent, changeless, eternal, free, infinite, and ineffable. There is also similar use of the analogical method in arriving at a proper theoretical understanding of the Absolute. *Via affirmationis, via negationis and via eminentiae* corresponds to *Adhyāsa or adhyaropa* (attempted prediction of Brahman using ordinary meanings of words), *apavidya* (negation or elimination of the finite meanings of these terms and culminating in *paramārtha-laksana* a legitimate supreme indication of Brahman). Analogy is an indication of the supreme reality without formally or properly defining it.

Though he compared Sankara and Aquinas, he said they were not simply saying the same thing in different ways. For Sankara the central focus is around realization of Brahman as one's true self, the liberating experience of the un-originated and non-dual ground as one's self. Aquinas was oriented to the free historical presence of the Divine to the human, culminating in a communion of persons in both love and knowledge. He was convinced of the compatibility of these two types of presence and went to declare that ontologically Christian personalism presupposed non-dualist metaphysics.

Sankara as *śṛutivādin*

Sankara's method of attaining experiential knowledge of Brahman is theological and he was essentially a *śṛutivādin*, scriptural based theologian. He was although quite capable of employing reason to argue his views and to destroy opposing ones ultimately he subordinated the power of rational thought to the authority of scriptural testimony. This synthesis of reason and revelation shared much with medieval Christian theology and only little with the European enlightenment. His attempt looks like making Indian thought as compatible with Christian thought. He studied Sankara, Ramanuja, K.C. Bhattacharya in conjunction with Augustine, Bonaventure and Aquinas. He was a leader in the philosophical encounter of Hindu and Christian thought and an inter-philosophical dialogue. For De Smet, Sankara's system was a pinnacle of all the metaphysical systems of India. Hindu reflective thought most perfectly attained to a correct metaphysical notion of a transcendent Absolute. He acknowledged the uniqueness of Sankara's contributions to the understanding of deity and world. Through careful study of Sankara, he had new ways of understanding and articulation of the interior presence of the Creator to the creature. De Smet was appreciated as the vedantin.

John Vattanky (1931 -)

A specialist in Indian system of logic, in Nyāya tradition, Vattanky has contributed significantly to enumerating the depth of Indian philosophical system from both epistemological and philosophy of language perspectives. Well acclaimed for his study on Gangesa's Navya-Nyāya system and Nyaya philosophy of God, he taught in JDV, Pune for number of years, involving in researches in Indian Christian thinking, publishing several scholarly works. His philosophical thought pattern is much shaped and influenced by system of Nyaya. Involving in depth level study of the basic texts of Navya-Nyāya, he interpreted and commented on various tenets of century old system of Indian logic and epistemology. As usually said, Nyaya system is alive only in academic cycles, scholars like Vattanky has made it revived in everyday discussions of Indian philosophical circles.

Taking forward the difficult and abstract Indian logical system of Nyaya into the realms of Religion and existence of God, as in theistic Nyaya, he applies how a sound logical and rational system could lead to other horizons of human quest in reaching beyond the known. Epistemological discourses need not necessarily stop with arriving at empirical knowledge alone but could take humans to self-understanding and cross over to the realms of the unseen and mystery. For him, Nyaya system of logic and epistemology and its theory of knowledge could also provide wider implications for the possibility of God-talk. The Absolute becomes the horizon of all efforts of rational enquiry through logic and epistemology. Such an application of reason in theistic discourses remains a counter argument for those who propagate that rationalism would lead to atheism. Denial of God and religion is sometimes promoted by having a recourse to logic and epistemology. As a contribution to Indian Christian thinking, Vattanky offers this profound purport of reason as to affirm theistic faith, as explicated in Navya-Nyāya system. As sound and valid argumentation leads humans not only to objective knowledge of things known and unknown, the self-understanding of humans themselves emerges as both knowing subject and the known object within. Consequently, epistemology helps humans understanding the metaphysical relation with the world, the other fellow human beings and the Absolute. Ontological principle of his very being is expressed as in both theoretical and existential levels. as a constitutive principle of his very being.

8.4. Thinkers Of Inculturation

Inheriting the two traditions, Indian and Christian some thinkers who could be at home in two traditions at a deeper level became extremely creative. Their Indianness enriched their understanding of Christian faith and their Christian vision enabled them to perceive things differently than non-Indian Christians.

D. S. Amalorpavadass (1932-1990)

As a multi-facteted thinker, Amalorpavadass made significant contribution to Indian Christian Thought, especially an experiential synthesis of Christian Faith and the Indian religo-cultural heritage. Program of and dialogue with other faith, are his central area of concern. He edited and authored several volumes. He brought down theology from academic heights and from isolation, to become a reality of everyday life of Indian Christian community. His writings breathe a sense of dynamism, reveal the importance of wholeness, integration and instill the imperative need of dialogue, inculturation and Indian spirituality.

God's revelation continues to take place even today through history. Various religious traditions are not opposed to each other. Understanding the scriptural traditions in other religions is to break new grounds, challenging the absolutism of the church in understanding Revelation and Salvation. Non-Christians have a place within God's plan of salvation. They do contain authentic spiritual and supernatural values which are the fruits of God's active presence. One cannot limit oneself to singularity of thought, since reality is varied and constantly changing. Pluralism is inevitable, given to the diversity of social, cultural, political and ideological realities, and given to the multiplicity of human situations and challenges. His keen sensitivity to God's ways in other traditions and cultures made him a profound thinker and promoter of dialogue and inculturation.

Bede Griffiths (1906-1993)

Establishing *Shantivanam*, a Christian ashram in Tamil Nadu, he made it become a center of contemplative life, of inculturation, and of inter religious dialogue. An ashram must be concerned with the 'search for God,' the continual effort to realize God, to discover the reality of the hidden presence of God in the cave of one's heart or depths of the soul. He goes beyond silence to stillness of heart. The earth-mother is the form of the ancient feminine found in rocks and caves and in the different forms in nature, the *shakti*, the divine power. His life is a marriage of East and West. He worked towards the rebirth of Christian wisdom in the light of the Vedanta, of non-duality, of the discovery of the inner self. He was a Christian in religion but a Hindu in spirit just as there are Hindus in religion while being Christian in Spirit, an assertion that can be the way of adapting the Christian faith to the local culture. His search is to go beyond the institutional structures of religion and discover the hidden mystery which is at the heart of all religion. He honored the sacredness of every person as unique image of the divine. Had a listening heart that was finely attuned to others and many came to open their hearts to him. His own profound wisdom and experience of the Christian Revelation interacted creatively with Hindu Vedanta.

Francis Xavier D'Sa SJ (1936 -)

A prolific writer, committed professor and sincere seeker, Francis X. D'Sa have expressed himself and his provoking thought on varieties of themes. Having done his doctoral studies in Indology with Gerhard Oberhammer at the University of Vienna, he taught in JDV, Pune. In addition to teaching and research activities in India, he regularly took up teaching assignments in Innsbruck, Frankfurt and, Salzburg, etc. He also founded the Institute for the Study of Religion in Pune, facilitating researches on cross-cultural ideologies, Indian Christian traditions, promoted interreligious and intercultural dialogues. His contribution to academic scholarly works ranged from classical Indian traditions of philosophy and religion to encountering other traditions. Taking forward Raimond Panikkar's cosmotheandric vision, he worked with a thirst for dialogue, harmony and integration. For him, in cosmotheandric understanding of reality, everything is interrelated and interconnected. Exhorting the persons who are used to their traditional practices and teachings without going deeper into their fundamentals, he shows them that 'self-centredness' and the 'chauvinism' of one's own tradition will give rise only to particularistic and exclusivist position. We need a global vision of interconnectedness. Only by crossing the borders one can discover wholeness.

Cross-cultural Horizons

Articulating the depths of his intuitive thoughts he is convinced that wholeness is achieved by consciously crossing the 'constructed' borders. One is not alone in this venture but with all engaged in their own way creative approaches in dealing with the problem of breaking the borders, ideologically, virtually created or imagined. "Borders have rarely fascinated me; on the contrary they have induced feelings of fear, anxiety, insecurity and in some cases, a sense of hopelessness." However, many borders one may cross, there still remain many more to be crossed, still to move out of the narrow confines, there is no end to crossing borders. "Our being flourishes every time we cross borders... we are essentially like the colors of the rainbow; our 'real' being compatible with borders." "To cross borders is to retrieve in some measure our originary state, is to come nearer to our authentic being." The cultural and religious boundaries are the most intransigent walls we face. He calls for change at the level of realm of meaning which is at the core of religion and culture and functions as the background for the process of being-and-understanding.

As borders are associated with personal and communal identity, he calls for making a distinction between the real identity and some fictitious ideological construct. The other is not perceived as the other but as the other side of one's own identity, because without the other the identity of one remains incomplete. In such sense, borders become barriers or bridges. Being-in-the world, makes us aware of being consciously present to oneself, and of knowing that there are no borders and then to cross over to being a subject relating with others. He proposes few *sutras,* as his theses, 1) The identity of persons - and their traditions – is an integral part of a network of interrelating identities. 2) The problem of identity becomes acute when the difference between identity and identification is overlooked. 3) On the ontological level identity is to be sought on the background of a primordial first person experience that we are. 4) The primordial first person experience that we are comprises the Cosmic, the Human and the Divine. 5) constant crossing of borders of the three dimensions is the direction in which wholeness, harmony, integration and peace are to be sought and found. The wholeness is achieved by inter-connecting three dimensions, by building bridges between two sides remaining in and retaining their specificities. "Bridges make crossing from one side to the other possible. A crossing is a going across a dividing line, making a cross. A bridge is across that which divides; in a way a bridge is a cross, a cross is a crossing over, a Pascha, a paschal mystery. To cross borders is to be on the way to the paschal mystery."

Dialogue & Inculturation

By end of the twentieth century, amidst ethnic disputes, sectarian violence and religious intolerance, we yearn for mutual understanding by dialoguing with others. Human beings are not just individuals but are essentially connected with the world of matter and mystery. Reducing dialogue to mere discussion of particular tradition, gives rise to a partial and one-sided approach that overlooks the organic interconnectedness and comprehensive understanding of religion and human reality. Holistic approach enables us to re-vision our understanding in the world of fragmentation where we are no more rooted to one place but in the process we have become uprooted, and unable to be at home anywhere. Religion as the integration of the Human with the Divine in the Cosmic is essentially a dialogue with reality. Both intrareligious dialogue (within one's own tradition) and inter religious dialogue (with other traditions) are interdependent. It would bring out the symphony of religions by correcting and complementing the individual traditions.

Proclaiming Christ in Asia is a part of evangelizing mission of the Church through witness, dialogue, inculturation and integral human promotion. As the gospel and evangelization are certainly not identical with culture, proclamation is dependent on culture. No entity is culturally free and there is no language which is culturally neutral. Every culture has its positive elements which are part of people's cultural heritage. A fruitful dialogue with the cultural and religious values of different people, is possible if each of the partners proclaim and listen to each other. It is through a process of not merely speaking and making others understand one's own position, but a process in which questioning, correction and complementarity have their place. "This is in no way a kind of relativism but a relativity of the expressions of our revelations." While Revelation itself remains absolute and eternal but its reception and proclamation are historically conditioned and culturally bound. The expression is not the experience. Faith is always experienced from within a definite perspective, a specific world-view and consequently faith-expressions are affected by their respective world-views. An effective proclamation needs cultural sensitivity.

8.5. Social Thinkers

Many Indian Christian thinkers devoted themselves in engaging with social issues affecting people and reflected on human liberation in specific contexts.

Arvind P. Nirmal (1936-1995)

He is one of those who thought, wrote and stood for the cause of the downtrodden, Dalits. Indian Christian thinking has ceased to be an enterprise of the elite and become an enterprise of peoples, Dalits, the broken, the torn, the rent, the burst; the split, the opened, the dispelled, the scattered, the downtrodden, the crushed, the destroyed, the manifested, the displayed. Every intellectual discipline has a social base. He advocates methodological exclusivism, not community exclusivism (Dalits need to be open to others). It is necessary because the tendency of all dominant tradition, culture or theology is to accommodate, include, assimilate and finally conquer other. As Dalits are considered to be *no people,* in dominant ideology, he affirms that they are *'real people.'* A search and expression of identity characterizes all liberative ideologies. Question of Dalit identity calls for a critique of Dalit historiography. As conquered people, they lost their history and the oppressors' history is imposed on them. Dalit studies should have a transforming liberative social vision with egalitarian social structures.

Dalit studies ground their theological affirmations in people's experiences of suffering. This pathos is prior to any involvement in struggle for liberation. It is in and through this pain-pathos that the sufferer knows God. Through this pain they know that God participates in human pain. It is in and through the weaker, oppressed and the marginalized that God's saving power is manifested, as brokenness belongs to the very being of God. God's divinity and humanity are both characterized by his Dalitness. He is one with the broken, suffers when people suffer, dies in his people's death and rises again in their resurrection.

Sathianathan Clarke

He gives a new ground by conceptually reimagining the relationship between Christianity and Dalits. Studying on the *paraiyars* of South India, he exposed the subjugated historical and religious themes. The term *paraiyar* essentially was a derivative of the Tamil word *parai*, drum. And it denotes people whose occupation was drum-beating. It is retained as memories of the ancient heritage, culture and religion of the *paraiyar*. Drum as it gathers together the strivings of subaltern communities, as an organizing symbol, represents the various features of the mode of thought and representation of morality. Drum conjoins both material and spiritual aspects of the mediation of Divine Blessedness. The drum as medium of Divine human communication that invokes, contains and dispenses divine power, the drum as an instrument of linking the subalternity of communities for resistive and emancipatory communal affirmation that exemplifies the solidarity of the human and divine in their resistance of human and demonic forces, and the drum as a symbol of manifesting and managing corporate suffering.

Felix Wilfred (1948 -)

He reflects on how Christianity can respond to various challenges of our times, dealing with various issues ranging from globalization, inculturation and human rights. We are faced with frightening developments of globalization and liberation that moves us to *amnesia of the poor* – the forgetfulness of the poor and their exclusion from our consciousness. The poor are told in many words that they are not wanted and they are a burden. Commitment to the poor and the marginalized, calls for a transformation of consciousness, by creating the spirit of servanthood, fostering a culture of solidarity, and creating critical consciousness. If globalization and liberalization benumb social consciousness, it is of utmost importance then we heighten critical consciousness in society for the protection of its victims. Respect for the marginalized and their legitimate rights cannot result simply from a general intellectual acknowledgement of the equality of all and its formulation in statements. Human right is to come from a deeper spiritual quest. Spirituality is basically a centrifugal movement, a movement away from the world of the self towards the other, and a movement towards truth that calls for a continuous transcendence of the self and its interests.

Towards Indian Christian *darśana*

Can we affirm that there has been emerging Indian Christian *darśana?* Indian Christians have a difference in philosophizing due to their twofold rootedness and given-ness of being Indian and Christian. As Indian Christians have experienced this diversity of looking at reality, plurality of faiths, how far they reflected on this Indian character is still an area to be explored. Indian Christian thinking is being channelized towards investigating into philosophical themes of social relevance. The contributions of the marginalized and minorities are tremendous. Often they have been overlooked by the dominant narrations. Indian Christian philosophizing needs to affirm the constitutive character of Indian Christianity. It needs to address both cultural and religious praxis of transforming the inequality in society and reshaping the society. It is a vision and a way of Indian Christian Philosophy. Social perspective needs to be an 'involved' philosophizing. Indian society in which Christians live has social structure with many subaltern groups that have experienced hardships, inequality, injustice, oppression, exploitation and domination. Indian Christian thinking has a responsibility for the subalterns. It is to open the flood gates of freedom and liberation for the neglected section of the society, tribal, Dalit, women and minorities. It is the responsibility of every philosopher to critically understand and assess the world in which one lives.

Chapter 9

MODERN-CONTEMPORARY INDIAN THINKERS A GENERAL ASSESSMENT

1. **Tradition and Modernity:** Contemporary Indian thinking as a movement had developed with a tension between 'tradition and change.' This tension seems to be at the core of the evolution of thought. An attempt at interpreting the process of thought from this view point seems to provide an excellent tool of analysis. This tension between traditionalists and modernists is found in the writings of each author or thinker of this period. Obviously some gave more importance to tradition, others to modernization. But, all embodied in their thought the basic tension between these two poles.
2. **Tradition: Static or Dynamic?** The root of this tension was found in the conflicting needs found in each individual as well as in society at large. An individual or a community needs continuity; without a sense of continuity one loses his identity and feels lost and overcome by situations, which go beyond his capacity to react in a constructive way. The individual and the community would collapse in total insecurity and loss of identity if it were not able to relate itself to a certain tradition. On the other hand, tradition tends to answer new situations with the solution meant for previous situations. Tradition without change becomes increasingly incompetent to answer new changes. When a society is faced by new problems it needs a capacity to change. Tradition has to be dynamic if it is not to become irrelevant. If the tradition does not find a way to transform itself, it tends to become more and more irrelevant. Those who cling blindly to such a tradition finds themselves increasingly unable to relate themselves to the world in which they live. In our course we will try to be sensitive to the

tension between tradition and change in the making of modern religious and philosophical thought.

3. **Indian Heritage: Criticism and Study:** Non-Indians criticized Indian religions when they encountered them for their external and popular forms and later began studying the deeper philosophical thought. One aspect of contemporary Indian philosophy is its more reflective evaluation of the traditions. After the Christian missionaries studying the Indian philosophical doctrines, the Veda, agamas and Tamil and Sanskrit, Scholars like Max Muller, Paul Deussen, A.B. Keith, G.U. Pope, Robert Caldwell and others discovered the historical and intellectual significance of this Indian heritage. These studies and translations revealed religious and philosophical similarities between Indian and European thoughts. Following them, Indian thinkers themselves began expounding the traditions and philosophies. Their expositions sound richer by the incorporation of new western developments.
4. **Anything New?** Because of the task of the orienting and of the re-orienting of the old and the new, contemporary Indian thought appears to be making little progress. But, if philosophy is understood as way of life and if the way of thought is to be adjusted to it and has to throw light on it, then philosophy cannot be completely new in any old culture. Although our theories can change quickly, human nature and historical cultures cannot be transformed so quickly.
5. **Constructive Interaction:** The most outstanding of the contemporary thinkers do not take in western ideas wholesale and indiscriminately, but ask themselves how the traditional philosophy of India is to be oriented towards the new doctrines and the new ideas of reality. These questions enable the philosophers to retain the spirit of traditional system and yet be conscious of the development in science and philosophy of the west. Almost all of them reconstruct the ancient philosophies after incorporating some doctrines from the west. Their work is not merely reaction or reconciliation, but also incorporation, cross cultural, inter-cultural enterprise.
6. **Revivalist Trends:** Contemporary thinkers of India, generally belonging to the vedantic traditions are focused very much. Some follow a particular tradition explicitly; others cull elements from different traditions.
7. **Can we say we have a contemporary *darśana*?** Contemporary concern is different from traditional contexts. Contemporary philosophizing cannot be just analytical assessment of traditional concepts and systems, or discussing on the relevance and significance of these concepts.

Finally, we find variety of thinkers from different fields ranging from social activism, politics, religion, academics, spirituality to subaltern emancipation.

As true to its character, India has produced reflective thinking, opposing and challenging the others and their traditions. It is discouraging to see that Indian thinkers have not been able to create a new system of thinking as their counterparts in the west during the same period of time. Serious questions rise in our minds of the inability of contemporary Indian thinkers in contributing newly to the world of philosophy. Contemporary Indian thinking mostly dealt with its own past and was caught up with its own socio-political assertions and negations. We are also concerned about the conception of 'glorious past' of ancient and classical India and the complacency of being struck with an idea that we have everything and we have said about everything. Where and how do we proceed from here?

SELECT BIBLIOGRAPHY

Ahhuwalia, B.K. *B.R Ambedkar and Human Rights*, Vivek Publishing Company, New Delhi,1981.

Ahir, D.C., The Legacy of *Dr. Ambedkar*, D.K. Publishers, Delhi,1990.

Ambedkar, B.R. *Writings and Speeches of Dr. Babasaheb Ambedkar.* Vol.1-17, Mumbai: Govt. of Maharashtra,

Ambedkar, Mahesh. *The Architect of Modern India - Dr. Bhimrao Ambedkar.* New Delhi: Diamond Books, 2005.

Anjan Kumar Banerji, ed. *Sarvepalli Radhakrishnan: A Centenary Tribute.* Benares: Benaras Hindu University, 1991.

Aurobindo. *The Future of Man.* Pondicherry: Aurobindo Ashram, 1970.

Aurobindo. *The Hour of God.* Pondicherry: Aurobindo Ashram, 1970.

Aurobindo. *The Life Divine.* Pondicherry: Aurobindo Ashram, 1970.

Aurobindo. *The Lights on Yoga.* Calcutta: Arya Publishing House, 1942.

Bali, D.R. *Modern Indian Thought.* Bangalore: Sterling Publication Pvt. Ltd. 1980.

Basak, Kokali. *Rabindranath Tagore: A Humanist.* New Delhi: Classical Publishing Company, 1992.

Bharathi K.S. *Foundations of Ambedkar Thought,* Dattsons Publications, 1990.

Bharathi, K.S. *Encyclopedia of Eminent Thinkers.* New Delhi: Concept Publishing Company,1998.

Brecher, Michael. *Nehru: A Political Biography*. London: Oxford University Press. 1959.

Chanchreek K.L. *Dr. B.R. Ambedkar: Patriot, Philosopher and Statesman* [Vol II] H.K. Publishers & Distributers, New Delhi, 1991.

Chaudary, Haridas. Ed. *The Integral Philosophy Sri Aurobindo.* London. George Allen and Unwin Ltd.1960.

Copley, Antony. *Gurus and Their Followers: New Religious Reform Movements in Colonial India.* New Delhi: OUP, 2000.

Dar, Bashir Ahamad. *A Study in Iqbal's Philosophy*. Lahore: Kashmiri Bazaar, 1948.

Dhawan, M. L. *Dr. S. Radhakrishnan.* Delhi: Bhavanan Prakashan, 1985.

Diehl, Anita. *Periyar E. V. Ramasamy: A Study of the Influence of a Personality in Contemporary South India.* New Delhi: B.J. Publications, 1978.

Drèze, Jean and Sen, Amartya. *Hunger and Public Action.* Oxford: Clarendon Press, 1989.

Fischer, Louis. *Gandhi His Life and Message for the World.* New York: New American Library Publication, 1954.

Gandhi, M.K. *The Story of My Experiments with Truth.* Ahmedabad: Navajivan Publication, 2005.

Gandhi, M.K. *An Autobiograpahy, Or The Story of my Experiments with Truth.* Tr. Mahadev Desai, Ahmedabad: Navaajivan 1927, Reprint 1998.

Gautam, C., *Life of Babasaheb Ambedkar*, Ambedkar Memorial Trust, London, 2000.

Gerard Hall, *Raimon Panikkar's Hermeneutics of Religious Pluralism*, Ann Arbor: UMI, 1994.

Grover, Verinder. Ed. *V.D. Savarkar,* Vol.14 of *Political Thinkers of Modern India.* New Delhi: Deep & Deep Publications, 1992.

Ilaiah, Kancha. *Post-Hindu India: A Discourse on Dalit–Bahujan, Socio-Spiritual and Scientific Revolution,* New Delhi: Sage Publications, 2009.

Ilaiah, Kancha. *Why I Am Not a Hindu: A Sudra critique of Hindutva philosophy. culture and political economy*. Calcutta: Samya, 1996.

Iqbal, Mohammad. *Reconstruction of Religious Thought in Islam*. London: Oxford University press, 1934.

J. Nicol, Farquhar. *Modern Religious Movements in India*. Delhi: Munshiram, 1967.

Keer, Dhananjay, *Dr. Ambedkar: Life and Mission.* Mumbai: Popular Prakashan, 1993.

Kumar Lal, Basant. *Contemporary Indian Philosophy.* New Delhi: Motilal Banarsidass Indological Publishers, 1978.

Mani, P. Mahajan & K.S Bharathi. *Foundation of Gandhi and Thought.* Nagpur: Dattsons Publication, 1987.

Manuel, Thomas. *The Advaita of Vivekananda.* Madras: T.R. Publications, 1991.

Massey, James. *Dr. Ambedkar: A Study of Just Society.* New Delhi: Manohar Publishers, 2004.

Mathur, Sobhag and Goyal, Shankar, eds. *Spectrum of Nehru's Thought*. New Delhi: Mittal Publications, 1994.

McDermott, Robert A. *Basic Writings of Dr. Radhakrishnan.* Bombay: Jaico Publishing House, 1981.

Mehta, Uday. *Modern Godmen in India: A Sociological Appraisal.* Mumbai: Popular Prakashan, 1993.

Moon, Vasant. ed. *Dr Babasaheb Ambedkar: Writings and Speeches.* Bombay: Education Department, Govt. of Maharashtra, 1989, 16 Vols.

Mumukshananda, Swami. *The Complete Works of Swami Vivekananda.*Vol. I-VIII, Calcutta: Advaita Ashram, 1991.

Naravana, V.S. *Modern Indian Thought.* Bombay: Asian Publishing House, 1967.

Nehru, Jawaharlal. *The Discovery of India.* New Delhi: Oxford University Press, 2000.

Nikhilananda, Swami. *The Gospel of Sri Ramakrishna.* Vol. I. Madras: R. K. Math, 1969, 1985.

Periyar E. V. Ramasamy: A Biographical Sketch. Chennai: The Periyar Self-Respect Propaganda Institution, 2004.

Periyar E.V.R, *Declaration of War on Brahminism.* Chennai: Dravida Kazhakam Publications, 1983.

Prasad, Ram Chandra. *Rajneesh: The Mystic of Feeling.* Delhi: Motilal Banarsidass.

Puthenpurackal, Johnson. *Raimon Panikkar, Being beyond Borders: A Commemorative Volume*, ed. Bangalore: Asian Trading Corporation, 2012.

Radhakrishnan, S. *Indian Philosophy.* Volume 1&2. London: George Allen & Unwin, Ltd., 1923.

Radhakrishnan, S. *The Hindu View of Life.* London: George Allen & Unwim, Ltd., 1927.

Raimon Panikkar, *Invisible Harmony,* Minneapolis: Fortress Press, 1995.

Raimon Panikkar, *The Cosmotheandric Experience*, New York: Orbis Books, 1993.

Raimon Panikkar, *The Intra-Religious Dialogue*, New York: Paulist Press, 1978.

Raimon Panikkar, *The Trinity and the Religious Experience of Man*, London: Darton, Longman & Todd, 1973.

Raimon Panikkar, *The Unknown Christ of Hinduism*, New York: Orbis Books, 1981.

Robin, Boyed. *An Introduction to Indian Christian Theology.* Madras: CLS, 1975.

Rodrigues, Valerian. ed. *The Essential Writings of B. R. Ambedkar.* Delhi: OUP, 2002.

Roy, Rammohan. *The English Works of Raja Rammohan Roy*. Calcutta: Sadharan Brahma Samaj, 1945-1958.

Sen, Amartya. *Choice, Welfare and Measurement.* Oxford: Basil Blackwell, 1982.

Sen, Amartya. Food Economics and Entitlements. Helsinki: Wider Working Paper 1, 1986.

Sen, Amartya. *Inequality Reexamined.* Oxford, Oxford University Press, 1992.

Sen, Amartya. *On Economic Inequality.* New York: Norton, 1973.

Sen, Amartya. *On Ethics and Economics*. Oxford: Basil Blackwell, 1987.

Sen, Amartya. *Poverty and Famines: An Essay on Entitlements and Deprivation.* Oxford: Clarendon Press, 1982.

Sen, Amartya. *The Argumentative Indian.* London: Allen Lane, 2005.

Sharma, Chandradhar. *A Critical Survey of Indian Philosophy.* New Delhi: Motilal Banarsidass, 1976.

Sing, Arya Krishan. *Swami Dayananda Saraswati: A Study of his Life and Work*. Delhi: Manohar, 1987.

Sinha, Sachidananda. *Iqbal, The Poet and his Message*. Allahabad: Ram Narain Lal Publishers, 1947.

Sinta, Jadunath. *Indian Philosophy, I.* Delhi: Motital Publishers Pvt. Ltd., 1999.

Srivastava, Rama Shanker. *Contemporary Indian Philosophy.* New Delhi: Munshiram Manoharlal Publishers, 1983.

Tagore, Rabindranath. *Gitanjali* (Song offerings). Madras: Macmillan India, 1992.

Tagore, Rabindranath. *Lipika: Prose Poems.* New Delhi: Clarion Books Publishers, 1978.

Tagore, Rabindranath. *Towards Universal Man.* New Delhi: Asia Publishing House, 1962.

Vahid, Syed Abdul. *Iqbal, His Art and Thought.* Lahor: Sheikh Mohammad Ashraf, Kashmiri bazaar, 1947.

Veeramani, K. ed. *Collected Works of Periyar.* Chennai: Periyar Self-Respect Propaganda Institution, 2004.

Veeramani, K. *Periyar and His Ideologies.* Chennai: Periyar Self-Respect Propaganda Institution, 1979.

Venugopal, P. *The Five-Pronged Battle of Periyar for an Egalitarian Society.* Chennai: The Periyar Self- Respect Propaganda Institution, 2005.

Vishwanathan, S. Narvan. *Modern Indian Thought.* New Delhi: Oriental Longman Limited, 1978.

Some Questions for Reflection

1. Describe the socio-religious situation of India in modern period.
2. What is the main contribution of the reformist Raja Ram Mohan Roy?
3. Describe the social significance of Dayananda Saraswati.
4. Describe the contribution of Ramakrishna
5. What is the significance of Vivekananda towards contemporary India?
6. What is the significance of Aurobindo towards contemporary India?
7. Describe the unique contribution of Tagore towards Indian freedom struggle.
8. Describe the contribution of Tilak towards Indian nationalism.
9. What is the significance of Savarkar towards contemporary India?
10. Describe the contribution of M. Gandhi
11. What is the significance of Nehru towards contemporary India?
12. What are the main insights of M.N. Roy
13. What are the main insights of E.V.R. Periyar
14. What are the main insights of Amartya Sen
15. Give the relevance of the subaltern thinker Ambedkar
16. Give the relevance of the subaltern thinker Mahatma Phule
17. Give the relevance of the subaltern thinker Narayana Guru
18. Give the relevance of the subaltern thinker Iyothee Thass
19. Describe briefly the contribution of S. Radhakrishnan towards Indian philosophy.
20. What are the salient aspects of Muhammad Iqbal's philosophy?
21. Give the basic vision of Ramana Maharishi
22. Give the basic vision of Jiddu Krishnamurthi
23. Give the basic vision of Osho Rajnessh
24. Give the basic vision of Sai Baba.
25. Mention briefly the contribution of Brahmabandhab Upadhyay

26. Mention briefly the contribution of Raimon Panikkar
27. Mention briefly the contribution of Richard De Smet
28. Mention briefly the contribution of Bede Griffiths
29. What is the Indian heritage?
30. Is tradition static?
31. What would be a Contemporary Indian *darṣana?*